ESCAPING THE
AMERICAN JOB TRAP

ESCAPING THE AMERICAN JOB TRAP

Creating Network Communities to Obtain Financial Freedom -

The Trend of the 21st Century

Dr. Ruby L. Ward, PhD.

To order additional copies of this book, contact:
Xlibris Corporation
1-888-7-XLIBRIS
www.Xlibris.com
Orders@Xlibris.com

CONTENTS

Is Your Job Secure??
Think Twice...

Or

Do You Think
You Can Get Rich
Working on a Job?...

Think Again...

THIS BOOK IS YOUR
BREAKTHROUGH
TO
A BETTER FINANCIAL LIFE

We live once on this earth and many people are living below
average salaries in a country where wealth and prosperity prevail

DISCLAIMER STATEMENT

FACTS

- The biggest concerns for most Americans today are job security and financial independence.

- Most people know that working on a job is the usual way to make a living, but less than one percent of individuals working on a job may get to financial independence.

- If you understand your purpose in life, you do not have to worry about job security due to the Spiritual Laws of Success.

- To obtain financial independence for their lives and families, a person must pursue other financial opportunities to create wealth other than total depending on a job.

Getting involved in financial opportunities offer alternative ways to create wealth, enjoy your family, help others, and have more leisure time.

- **This book will led you to living a successful financial life.**

This book is about living your dreams.

ACKNOWLEDGMENTS

I thank God, Our Lord and Savior, for giving me the vision and desire to write this book. This book came to me in a vision to help people escape the American job trap and obtain financial freedom. God not only inspired me to write this book, but the Lord gave me a plan, through network marketing, to create wealth outside of job dependence. You may have been involved in a network marketing company once before and got negative results, but cheer up and don't give up on network marketing. This book will change your life.

I thank my staff and other friends for encouraging me to write this book. I thank my husband who has been very instrumental in helping me to share my ideas and put together a plan to help other people. I thank my son, daughter, son-in-law, daughter-in-law, and sisters. I thank my mother and father for leading me to accept the Lord at an early age. I thank the editor and publisher for making this book available for other people.

Finally, I thank my network marketing business partners who encouraged and inspired me to write this book.

INTRODUCTION

This book is about understanding ways to create wealth by taking advantage of other financial systems to live a better life other than working on a job to "escape the American job trap." People should be made aware that there is an economic system "call a job" already in existence for every person financial life that does not have a vision or have taken the initiative, time and responsibility to establish and control their own livelihood. This book will help you get on course with your life through God. It will show you why you are struggling financially and why you will never be able to get out of debt and live a financially secure life as long as a job is your only source of income. Statistics based on families' incomes indicate that many American families are still living in bondage to its system even though America's business philosophy is based on a free enterprise system, where there is the potential for everyone to accumulate wealth. This is because a free enterprise system is based on creating wealth through ownership or investment; not by working a job, which coincide with God-given plan to obtain wealth. Too much emphasis has been put on a job as the only stable source for the average person to make a living. This is why so many people are on welfare, struggling, committing crime, and not able to get out of debt because they have become dependence upon a system of working for someone else. This is fine for those people who enjoy working on a job, but our government must put equal or more emphasis on ownership and self-employment for obtaining money other than training for a job for those individuals desiring to be independence of the system to better their life. Working on a job is the reason why many people are struggling and is one of the majors hinders to keep a person from obtaining prosperity in life. The question is "Who enjoys struggling or living on a tight budget all their life?"

This is why this book is so important as a guide to lead you and your family to financial independence in the New Millennium. This book is not about a get rich quick scheme to avoid working, but rather to help you identify with your dream, focus your attention, and catch a vision for your life and take advantage of other financial opportunities in life to obtain abundant wealth. This book helps you to escape the normal traditional job pattern of working on a job to make a living. When you work on a job for someone else, it hinders you from achieving your purpose in life. In addition, you, also, receive a salary, based on a fixed income, which is not enough to pay variable monthly bills. This is how jobs limit people's growth and prevent them from achieving unlimited income. We want people to recognize the impact of the preexistence economic system it has on their lives. Then make a decision to move from a job to a self-employed system to transform the socio-economic well being of your life financially, forever, as God has intended for man to live. Today, there is a lot of information and emphasis being placed on getting out of debt, but only a few people have touched on the root problem that prevents people from being in debt today and back in debt tomorrow. The key issue is that it takes a lot more money now days for the families to survive, and the medium income per family is well below the normal standards of living. We are not talking about a lot of spending just to be spending, but buying what you need and having some money left for investing or to take a vacation without worrying about how the bills are going to be paid.

To accomplish this, you need to understand your current financial position and get a vision for creating money. One of the ways to get out of debt or survive in the New Millennium is by taking advantage of various companies' marketing plans through alternative marketing opportunities, which are designed to produce unlimited income. The debt ratio is high and still rising in a nation where abundant wealth is plentiful. We can all feel the impact of changes in our economy created by the technology industry. Starting a business venture with various network marketing companies can help you eliminate debts and will play an ever–expanding role in your finances in the New Millennium. The technology movement is here and has forever changed the way business is conducted and marketed. The paradigm of having an increase in the number of people working on a traditional job as before in the past will decline due to the increase of small business owners.

Today, you should be asking yourself, "am I prepared to live in the new global world and be financially equipped to handle the changing situations that will affect me and my family?" What are you doing in your life spiritually and financially to meet the layoffs and other physical changes now occurring in today's job market?

Life is a cycle and relies on making effective choices concerning changes in your livelihood spiritually, physically, and financially. However, we find people unprepared and not ready for change. In America, there are far too many people merely existing in life and living one day at a time without a purpose or mission for their life to fulfill a need in the world. Thus, they do not allow variation or effective changes to occur or take place in their lives. As with most changes, it affects a person's spiritual and socio-economic well being. If people do not have a means or a vision for obtaining or making money, there is no way for them to survive physically and materially in this world. If you want to have abundant life, you got to have a vision for obtaining it. The technology movement has created one of the biggest visions in our lives, and many people have not capitalized on the opportunity. The technology movement affects every person in three distinct ways. Firstly, it eliminates some dependence from working on a "job." Secondly, it creates new opportunities to obtain wealth, and thirdly, it has caused too many people to lose their jobs. This movement has affected both skill and unskilled laborers, but the greater impact was on unskilled laborers, who have no alternative ways of earning a living without working on a job. This is due to the America's job training and preparation system, and many people are so comfortable and brainwashed into believing that being employed with a job is the only legal source to earn a living, and to escape this paradigm is to retire or die. Then, of course, after retirement, retirees find that they don't have sufficient income to survive. In response, they continue to work to make ends meet and find themselves back in the American job trap,—struggling to survive again. The most devastating aspect about working on a job after retirement, is that doing post–retirement most people are mentally unprepared to succeed at anything else. Therefore, many people become employed in service jobs; such as working at retail stores, auto shops, gas stations, etc. These retirees generally receive minimum wages, no matter how many years of experience or college education they have. Many educated retirees in higher job positions usually pursue self-employment in consulting services or as an independent contractor. As we have seen in the past, corporate America and high tech-companies usually release their employees when they reach age 40. In corporate America, this is generally done to avoid paying their employees' retirement compensation. The government, however, will allow their employees to stay on the job until retirement with meaningless work to do. In the future, we will see fewer people being hired by the government and large corporations for jobs at the past rate due to the rapid expansion of the technology movement. This is why, you should take steps to establish your own financial future if you are one of those employees.

Because of the advancement of technology, more and more, companies and individuals are marketing their services and products from the Internet. The Internet is creating opportunities of all types for people in need of a vision for their life. As we progress into the future, we will see more companies and people coming into compliance with this movement. Individuals should be aware that companies are still training and hiring, but this does not guarantee that you will have a job or job security, because there will be few corporate jobs available. The technology age supports a wireless society, forming network-marketing teams, and self-employment businesses on the Internet through network marketing mergers, affiliate programs, and establishing partnerships. If you or your company are not part of a network that manufacture products and services; distribute services that are involved in telecommunications and utilities; handles waste management; invents electronics; or networks as an Internet provider or consultant, then you should get a vision to become involved in marketing distribution. I challenge you to take the initiative to get a vision and get involved in some aspect of technology to live a debt free life if you are seeking to gain wealth. Otherwise, you will be left behind because the words for the 21st century are "Network" and "Wireless". Technology is the trend of the future so your vision should be to develop a need in that area.

Most of the tasks and jobs formerly done by large corporations and the government are being, and will continue to be, contracted out to mid-size and small businesses that have merged, and to home-based businesses that are growing rapidly. Traditional and professional jobs are becoming very few, unpredictable, and unreliable. It would be wise not to become totally dependent on any job as the only "source" of income since self-employment will be the financial source for families in the future. Getting involved with self-employment opportunities, network marketing companies, and teaming with other small companies to obtain the expertise that you do not have, is the way of the future. The two greatest advantages of the technology movement are being able to create an explosion of wealth and the development of the Internet. The Internet has created many millionaires and billionaires. Most companies are conducting business from their Internet web site. Timing is very critical and important in the technology movement because technology changes are rapid and unpredictable. Also, timing is a very critical factor for a person to identify an opportunities to create wealth and pursue it quickly. The small businesses and Internet network opportunities that are here today will be gone tomorrow. Another advantage of technology is giving value to the words "Networks" to create wealth. This is why it is recommended that you become involved in some facet of network marketing. It doesn't matter what your career status or position, it would benefit anyone to take an active part in the explosive areas of network marketing distribution, multilevel-marketing, or direct selling opportunities since it is part of the Internet explosion.

Recent trends show a dramatic-increase in the amount of people involved-and the amount of revenue generated through sales by direct-network marketing on the Internet. Statistics show that even many people in high profile occupations, such as–lawyers, doctors, and professional football players, are involved in network marketing, and are marketing their businesses from the Internet as shown in various business magazines. The approach that some professionals have in common is that they have created a network of specialized personnel. These professionals are aware of how to make money and they understand the pooling of individual investments and people to build a financial network by purchasing products and services from each other, and in return for obtaining financial independence and more control of their time.

Due to technology, many people have and will continue to worry about losing their jobs, but I believe the technology movement is one of the greater things that could have happened. It forces people to find a vision and/or purpose through inventions, and it affords people an opportunity to be set free from poverty conditions and escape the penalty of financial bondage by working for another person. In addition, technology has created a total new type of work, which allow a person to escape the job trap of traditional employment by exercising the benefits of the Internet and self-employment. This is why this book is called "Escaping the American Job Trap". The traditional job system has supported an economic system of job-control with little of no effort and respect on the part of another individual to be compensated for work performed to meet financial obligations. Our economic system encourages men to work for another man without putting equal emphasis on pursuing ownership through investments. Thereby, creating a "Lazy Man Syndrome". More information on this term is explained in Chapter 2, page 60 and Chapter 3, pages 109, 110, and 111.

To be in control of your life, applied knowledge and the use of information are essential, so you will not find yourself being controlled by the system. Unless we do something or take responsibility for our life, it will not change for the better. It will continue to evolve as a clock in a circuitous sphere promoting poverty, lack, welfare, and governmental control.

Too many people are on welfare, not because they choose to be there, but rather, it is because our economic system supports getting an education. Then seeking employment from another individual as the ultimate source of making a living. As you can see, the American labor force system promotes and supports the Lazy Man Syndrome by working for someone else, and it does not allow a person the opportunity to be all they can be in life. Our system takes advantage of those people who are less ambitious and motivated to change their lives. However, we cannot blame any one, not even ourselves, for an economic system that supports or perpetuates both hope and despair, which has caused 80 percent or more people to fall into the job trap. We have been inundated with the philosophy that we must work a traditional job, in order to function as productive citizens and have an abundant life. The only other option given to people and job rejects is to enroll in the welfare system. The welfare system has been the biggest detrimental system, as it has undermined and cheated many men and women from achieving their vision or purpose in life, because it has allowed and supports despair and poverty.

Working on a job or being on welfare has never allowed people to achieve their ultimate potentials alone. A job has been the way of life for about 80 percent of American people until their retirement or death based on vital labor statistics. This is the way we have been taught, and as a result many people's dreams have been shattered. It is only through the grace of God and His Holy Spirit and through His power that we have been surviving. Every individual was created equal, with purpose, and was given abilities from God to live an abundant life. Most people don't understand that human beings were created in the physical form on earth to fulfill a God-given purpose, which is Divinity in its essence. It takes a divine human form to fulfill a purpose, according to the "Seven Spiritual Laws of Success," written by Deepak Chopra. In his book, Dr. Chopra, "states that we all have unique talents and a unique way of expressing these talents to meet our needs." By being spiritually connected to God, we can use these talents to fulfill our needs and create unlimited wealth and abundance. Therefore, if a person wants to achieve purpose in their life, first they must fulfill a need. This is how you can find your true potential and purpose for life. Prophet Vaugman Jarrold states "where there is no vision, needs are not fulfilled, and where there is no purpose known, abuse is ineviable."

One of the greatest benefits of the technology movement is, firstly, to provide a need, a challenge, and an opportunity to retrain the minds; especially, of those individuals desiring to move from working on a job to owning a business. If the average American does not understand this, he will be left behind. The rich will get richer and the poor will get poorer. This is why this book must be read and information shared with others, so they can make sound decisions and understand how to change their financial situation.

Secondly, the technology movement endorses network marketing because it is a " vision" of building relationships to obtain wealth. Relationship building is what the Bible is about and endorses, and it is very much based on the principles of a free enterprise system (America, one Nation under God with liberty and justice for all). Marketing products and services is the catalyst behind a free enterprise system of fulfilling needs for survival, physically and financially. Therefore, many companies whether traditional or conventional are involved in "networking" to a certain degree for the purpose of marketing goods and services; and, of course, for finding and rewarding people to perform the work.

Network marketing has been around for many years as a vision for obtaining wealth. Some people have found and achieved their purpose in life financially through networking and helping others. Some of the billion dollar companies associated with network marketing opportunities are Amway, Mary Kay, and Shaklee that have been around for years and are still offering home-based business opportunities to people as a way to obtain unlimited wealth through their distribution system. Far too many people shy away from network marketing programs whether they are offered an opportunity to participate in a business venture or not. However, for those companies that do have a vision for network marketing, thank God for them allowing people to invest in their marketing programs. This creates a WIN-WIN situation for them as well as for the independent contractors or distributors. These companies have a "vision" of creating wealth for the ordinary people. A person is offered an opportunity to escape working on a job with a high rewarding compensation and incentive programs that produces financial independence by getting other people involved in the companies. The network system works best where a large number of people pool a small investment in a company and receive a rights to market that company's product and services mostly through word of mouth. More and more companies in telecommunications networks and health care services originating today are catching the " vision" of offering similar opportunities for individuals to achieve wealth as never before in history. All the people have to do to get out of debt is catch the "vision" offered by network marketing.

Statistics from direct sales reports show that these companies have proven that network marketing is a sound and stable market-ing 'vision" that produces phenomenal income that has changed the lives of ordinary people forever. The birth and time for net-work marketing to soar will be the 21st Century the (Network Generation), and most people still have limited understanding of what comprises the basic nature of this type of marketing. This, coupled with past negative publicity and limited number of suc-cessful people, has caused many people to not invest in network marketing companies as an alternative source to create income. Like every system, it has its risks and downfalls, but this doesn't make it wrong or illegal. Network marketing is a legal way to generate wealth. If more people understood the basic principle of how wealth is created through a network marketing business as an independent contractor or distributor, more people, especially minorities, would get a "vision" in network marketing to produce financial independence to replace their job. I participated in a franchise conference in Washington, DC, in 1999, and statistics was presented that showed 3.6 percent of firms in the U.S. are black-owned versus 96.4 percent of firms white and others-owned. The major reason that the average person including minorities do not understand the "vision" of network marketing as a natural way to earn a living is because they don't understand the total concept of investing into a business to make money. A job is considered as their "vision" and as the only natural way to earn a living because their minds have already been trained and programmed to work and to earn money by a job. Working on a job is not the employee's vision, it is the employer' vision. Another reason is that the black families have always been workers from slavery and this mentality or "fault vision" has been passed down from generations to generations. Very few homes in the black race can attest to owning their own businesses that were passed down to the next generation that could be duplicated to create wealth. On the other hand, the majority of the people see no risks associated with a fixed income. To them, this is guaranteed money to pay their bills. Because of these reasons when people can't pay their bills, they usually get on welfare, so this becomes a reality to them. This is why very little effort has been made by minorities to exploit networks, the internet, or network marketing opportunities as a sound business investment on a large scale as it has been in the past. If the government would emphasize helping people to start network-marketing businesses, poverty would vanish.

Today, more knowledge and awareness are being circulated through books, and magazines; such as *Fortune* 500, Black

Enterprise, and Success are promoting "creating wealth" and ranking network-marketing companies because they see the growth potential and connection with the Internet as the financial wave of the future. We have seen large companies merging together to form strategic alliances with network marketing companies to distribute their products and services by removing the middleman, middle level staff, and the traditional sales force. Thus, the network marketing companies pass these savings to the average consumers as opportunities with a lucrative compensation plan. The evolution of technology via the Internet is changing the way business is now being conducted, distributed, and marketed. Because of poor publicity and the lack of knowledge in the past, the average person would not take advantage of network marketing opportunities, until more large corporations adapt to this type of system. My recommendation for any person seeking financial independence is to find a network-marketing company, and become a part of the technology movement to create variable income rather than fixed income. Finding a company that promotes network marketing and investing into their distribution system, and promoting product or services on the Internet is something everybody can do with a small investment, the proper planning, and training.

The Internet is the vehicle of the New Millennium, which people are using to acquire information, market and sell both products and services to the consumers, and–thus, hereby, creating a paperless society. The Internet will play a valuable role in the way network marketers conduct business because people can signup with companies on the Internet, reach large number of people, and fulfill order requests within 24—48 hours or less. The Internet will offer network-marketing distributors a way to involve more people and also provide a faster medium. Because of the Internet, many companies have abolished their sales staff and have instead contracted the sales of services and products to network marketing companies. The Internet, which is the advancement of technology, creating small businesses and contracting-out services and products, is a major reason for downsizing and reengineering of jobs. With the Internet and the cutting back of traditional jobs, there is no job security. This creates a greater risk of loss for a person working in organizations, large and small companies, including the Government, who is depending on their weekly salary. Since all jobs are at risk, more and more people are taking serious steps to finding other sources to protect their financial obligations and are becoming involved with network marketing companies and starting their small and home-based businesses, which is the gateway to future careers.

People are hunger for wealth satisfaction and are seeking both opportunities and jobs that will create enough money to pay their bills and have extra money left for leisure activities. Therefore, for those people in search of finding a source of creating wealth that offers financial independence, try network marketing, which is in demand. Individuals are giving up their professional careers after attaining extraordinary wealth through network marketing distribution.

Network marketing opportunities have and will continue to attract professional people; mainly, because they have caught a vision. This "vision" is about having shorter working hours and the innately lucrative potential of network marketing, which in turn affords them the opportunity to have more income with less stress and more quality time with their families. We also read about some middle-class income individuals who are catching the vision and are earning in one month what they made in a year working on the job. Also, there are testimonies from individuals on welfare who have discovered that they can build a network of wealth in their homes without an extensive education.

Virtually, any one can get involved in network marketing ventures since there are no special requirements needed to qualify, as a job. The major qualification is a person having a vision to change their financial future. The seven secondary qualifications needed are the ability to follow directions, discipline, a trainable attitude, a strong desire to change one's life, a desire to help others, determination, and perseverance. As with the traditional jobs, most network marketing companies have their own training program. The biggest "vision" for becoming involved with a network marketing company is that it offers a person the opportunity to become a business owner at the least time devoted to the effort and to take advantage of tax deductions. Being self-employed is very imperative to living in a free enterprise country and in control of your finances.

This book is design to influence, stimulate your thinking, and help you to understand "vision" and to catch a vision for creating money for your life to achieve unlimited income. In addition, my staff will help anyone with a vision seeking to become involved in a network-marketing, other small businesses, or investments to help you have a better financial future. You might have gotten involved in the wrong opportunity in the early developmental stages of a network marketing companies and lost your investment and interest, because the company failed to achieve its goal. However, if this should happen to you, it is best not to speak negative and to give up your vision for network-marketing companies. You should keep evaluating and fishing for the right opportunity in network marketing to come into existence. Before most people learn to ride a bike, they fall at least 3 to 4 times and become more determined, wiser, and try again. This is with everything, and there are going to be some trials and tests until the goal is accomplished. Also if your are seeking success, "failure will usually comes before success." and, the right company to get involved with is looking for you, the self-motivated person with a "vision" seeking an opportunity. **Failure is not for you to quit, but it is the first step to reaching success**. Do your research and become wiser in selecting a network marketing company or any venture that will change your financial status. Network marketing is reaching its peak stage on the Internet. Are you a part of it? Opportunity to obtain wealth through network marketing must be matched with the right person, company, products, and services. Further information on how to select, evaluate and choose a good network marketing company will be in chapter 2, page 61 of this book.

Some of the information in this book is repeated to stress a specific topic or to clear up any negative viewpoints about network marketing and self-employment as ways to generate wealth. We want to help you get financial secure by presenting positive information toward network marketing as a business opportunity for everyone with a vision seeking financial independence, and it is a legal opportunity to earn extra income to meet your financial challenges. Don't give up on life by not being able to find a job and succumb to drugs or crimes as the only alternatives to make money. Get a vision for your life and run with it and there are people to help you. Be sure to write down the vision on paper, aim at the farthest goal, find others to share the vision, and you will achieve it. For example, **the vision for getting involved with a network marketing company should be to create money for you and others through a team approach**. I believe getting involved with the network marketing's vision can create extraordinary wealth in a short length of time. The lack of vision for such a strong, powerful plan to achieve wealth led me to write this book. I believe that building a network marketing organization has the same powerful outcome as produced by the people in Babel as shown in the Bible in Genesis 11:1-9, where the people of Babel were building a tower of one language on earth for a negative reason to control the universe. In verse 6, the Lord said, "let me go down and see what is happening and the Lord said, "Behold they are all "one" (meaning that they were in unity. The people were in agreement and in large numbers), and now nothing will be restrained from them, which they have imagined to do." The Babel's people had a "vision" and other people joined with the same vision and nothing would have been able to stop them from achieving their purpose or goal. The key words seen in these passages were a need, vision, oneness, unity, desire, benefit, agreement, relating, teaming, commitment, perseverance, determined, motivated, courage, recruiting, believing, expecting, and reality. However, the Babel's vision was for the wrong reason, and the Lord was the only one able to stop them from achieving their goal. This was a strong form of network marketing that was created for a cause. The same power produced in this situation would be generated for any network marketing opportunity, **if you can get a group of committed people together for the same purpose, they can not be stopped from achieving their goal of financial independence by networking or whatever the cause.** The Babel's vision was for a negative achievement. How much more would a positive vision prevails?

CHAPTER 1–IN SEARCH OF THE AMERICAN DREAM

Taking Control of Your Financial Life

All of my life I have been in search of the American Dream. I went to college to get an education as my mother had told me because this was her vision for me to have a better life. She knew that by my going to college, I would be presented with challenges and opportunities to improve my life. I enrolled in college, became a high school teacher, and later became a Federal government employee. I admit that college did give me an opportunity to be more selective about choosing the type of job I wanted. Since I had a job with the Federal government, I believed I was off to the greatest opportunity that life had to offer to an individual. Because of my college education, I was offered a higher-level income position as opposed to individuals who didn't have a degree. I climbed the corporate ladder very quickly. Later in my career, I went back to school to get an advanced degree. Now, I have received my Doctorate Degree in Divinity and I'm still working on a job, but the good part is that I know now what it takes to obtain the American Dream and to be financially secured.

Upon graduating from college and working on a job for someone else I realized that this would not afford me the opportunity to become financially secure. This is a true statement for the majority of the college graduates who get a job working for someone else, and they are like every ordinary person still struggling to earn a sufficient income to make ends meet and to have enough money remaining to live their dreams. Nevertheless, college is one of the best ways to increase your knowledge and to create individual growth, discipline, and it offers an opportunity to choose the best traditional career in life. However it is important for you to know that college alone will not create money or financial independence if this is your reason for attending college. If you attend college and your main purpose is to have a better financial future, then you need to focus your study in entrepreneurship. This is an area that offers you self-employment opportunities to obtain the skill and knowledge of becoming a business owner rather than seeking a job as employment to become financially independence.

The key to financial independence is to get involved in a career that offers the opportunity for your money to work for you, instead of you working for money.

America's economic structure is based on a free enterprise system. Working for someone else contradicts this principle if you are seeking financial freedom. To benefit from a free enterprise system, a person must have a vision to become a business owner (an employer vs. an employee). Another term used is self-employment. We will see more and more people becoming self-employed as we continue to move from an industrial society to a technological society (marketing information and services via the Internet). To the individual, this means that the way to earn money is also changing as we witness to more jobs being abolished through reengineering and downsizing. During the past decade, it has been reported in various business reports and magazines that over 9 million people have been laid off their jobs and this figure is expected to arise as we move further into the New Millennium. For many of us, this change has been painful since so many Americans have lost their jobs, and some, not expectantly. More job layoffs are expected due to the technology conversion. "Unfortunately, the loss of these jobs is not temporary, nor is it part of a typical business cycle. Most of the jobs lost in the last decade will not return," as written by Michael S. Clouse and Kathie Jackson Anderson in their book "Future Choice." These layoffs not only affect the blue and white-collar workers, but everyone. The technology movement coming into existence will lead to more lost jobs and to more people pursuing the American Dream through self-employment. This is because the technology age is more in tune with a free enterprise society concept.

Of all the career choices in America, statistics supports the concept of self-employment, owning your own business, is the number one opportunity to offer financial freedom for all unless an inheritance occurred. In the American's economic system, under free enterprise, there will always be the super rich and the poor based on the attitude and choices a person makes. Already in America, we see a lot of people who do not want to take the responsibility to start a business because they perceive it as a lot of work, and they like a job better. Too many, the labor force is foreseen as an easy way to make a living with less risk, and 80 percent of the people in America have programmed their minds to work, and they are set to work for a living until retirement. This is their "vision", mind set, thinking, and way of life for many workers in America of how to make money, and you can't do anything to change their thinking even if you gave them a business. Some people are this way and they like to be told what to do and how to do it. This is called "structure conditioning" and they move in action as a robot and there is nothing you can do to get them to change. In the New Millennium, technology is the driving force behind our economy, and is creating opportunities for everyone to obtain extraordinary wealth regardless of their educational background or race. However, you must get purged into an opportunity system offering a financial vision to change your future.

One thing we must understand from a business aspect is that **the American economic system is built on the concept of marketing to achieve life's goal.** Whether, you are working on a job, for someone else, or operating your own business, you are involved in some aspects of marketing. Helping people is marketing. Home-based businesses will continue to be birthed in America due to a free enterprise society and the technology era. The companies, we once thought we could depend on for job security, are consolidating and merging. Most new jobs in America will be service related-jobs and through technology on the Internet. "Most of the manufacturing jobs that were formerly in America are now in Mexico or overseas. Since 1965, U.S. corporations have built more than 1,800 plants–which employ more than 500,000 workers—in neighboring Mexico alone. That figure is expected to climb to almost 3,000 plants by 1995, according to projections by the Secretariat of Commerce and Industrial Development in Mexico City. While they say they regret the impact on U.S. workers, companies as diverse as Zenith and Fisher-Price, say they have no choice, but to move to countries where wage rates are lower if they want to remain competitive," according to Michael S. Clouse and Kathie Jackson Anderson, in "Future Choice."

For those Americans who do not want to move to another country to work on manufacturing jobs, then the ultimate choice is to start a home-based business or get involved in network marketing business. Otherwise, the only potential to find employment would be in such places as restaurants, hospitals, or department stores. There will be jobs available in the government, but not as numerous as before. Because of the changes taking place, people should take the initiative to get as much knowledge as they can about the computer and the Internet. This will better position them as a user of the computer and for job placement is the rigors of the new market place.

Recently, home-based businesses are increasing in distribution of products and services through network marketing, direct selling, or multi-level marketing. With very little experience, these people are finding new ways to market their businesses on the Internet without depending on friends and family members as before and are receiving unbelievable income. Because of the changes taking place on the Internet to help you reach a greater depth of people to market products and services, a business in network and direct marketing needs to be considered in great depth for any person seeking financial independence. This book should help to understand the wisdom behind network marketing/direct selling opportunities as a vision to financial freedom to escape the American job trap and to have your money work for you. But keep in mind, you may or may not have built an organization in the past or have gotten negative reactions from direct, network, or multi-level marketing, because it was new and most people did not treat it as a business. Some people tried to use the traditional marketing approach (as a single salesman business) to build direct-marking organizations, but this cannot be done successfully. This is one of the major reasons why network/direct marketing has not been unsuccessful for many people, and also because the people didn't have a vision about how money is created and to build teams.

Network/direct marketing is a pure team approach where people's effort is leveraged and duplicated to produce high income in which all are paid vs. being paid on a single person's marketing efforts. In the past, more individuals have been able to build organizations in network/direct marketing by seeing the vision and bring determined. Although teams were built, however, there was no security or loyalty to the business organization, and this is not what network marketing is all about. As we move into the 21st century, we will see more people getting involved with network marketing opportunities, because they will not have a choice, unless they move to Mexico or overseas to work in factory jobs, as discussed earlier. Network marketing opportunities deserves more respect than it is getting due to the negative connotations of dealing with a force of untrained people. Network/direct marketing, if operated correctly, will create for you an extraordinary income with shorter working hours and enjoyable work.

The only excitement about working on a job is that you meet beautiful people as yourself. Some people are in the same predicament that you are in and are looking for opportunities to earn a better living besides working on a job to obtain money. The Federal government workers conversations are usually, "Who got that promotion? Who is getting that job? Who is retiring?" "Thank God it is Friday" and "it is Monday, four more days to go." Many Federal workers are on a list, waiting for someone to retire to get their next promotion. This is their vision until they retire or die. Their vision is to work for money. Life should be more than working on a job every day to earn a living. The old saying, "if you don't work, you don't get paid."

One day while on the job, I started thinking about life. Should life be more than just working every day for money and caught in the rat chase? I said, "Lord, I must have missed something in life!" To work nine hours a day for a paycheck, and after all bills are paid, there is hardly enough leisure money left. Another thing that concerned me about a job is the routine working schedule–off on Friday and back to work on Monday and no time to enjoy family and life. Then I heard the voice of the Lord say, "As long as you work for money, it will always be like that under the control of someone else."

I am about to retire, and like most retirees, I have been relying upon my job, social security, pension plan, and personal savings. I wonder will there be enough money in retirement for me to live a good life. So, often I have seen many senior citizens get another job after retirement to survive, and do not live a quality life style for enjoyment.

Past experiences and obtaining knowledge on how money is created have helped me to save enough money to live a quality life style and to get involved in investments where money can work for me. Also, being married has kept me from working on two jobs (full-time and part-time). The point I am trying to make is that when most people retire, if they have not taken steps to invest or save some money in a 401-K plan, they will have to continue to work a job to survive until death. This is happening now to most people when they retire, and this will continue for the American labor force. The only way to escape the "American job trap" is to be accountable and responsible and take action to control your life by investing into mutual funds, starting a business, or getting involved with a network marketing companies. These steps are what people should take at the beginning of their career life thirty years ago. The key to having an effective financial life is getting a "vision" for your financial future and learning to leveraging your time and money.

Twenty years ago someone introduced me to a network/direct marketing opportunity, and I got involved in Shaklee Products as a distributor. I knew this was an alternative way to become financially independent. I was very happy about the new venture because I saw myself becoming financially independent and leaving my job so I could be home with my children. I knew that I couldn't get wealthy by working on a job, but I never knew the reason why. After I sought the Lord, twenty years later I was told that I was working for money instead of money working for me. Therefore, I got involved with several investments (see pages 81-87).

I tried to build my business and get others involved, but the friends I shared this with, could not see the vision. Most of my friends were comfortable working on a job for money and associated network-marketing opportunity to being a pyramid scheme. This was just an excuse not to join. I later realized that they were trapped into their jobs, making ends meet; and therefore, didn't want to disturb their comfort zone. I didn't think about network/direct marketing again until 1994, when someone introduced me to LCI, Inc. LCI is a telecommunications company, later named changed to Quest, offers commission and residual income on long distance telephone use. This opportunity was made possible due to the deregulation of the telecommunications industry, an act passed by the Federal Trade Commission. Many of LCI's distributors were making more in a month than I was making in a year. I joined as a distributor and got off to a successful start by getting other people involved. I was excited because my money had started to work for me. I was receiving a check every month and this was what I had wanted in life. By the time the checks started rolling in, AT&T dropped their telephone rate as an effort to regain their customers since so many of their customers were joining LCI. In addition, AT&T started offering their previous customers a check ranging from $25—$150 or more for people to switch back to their telephone service, and this was a war. Based on AT&T marketing strategy, I started losing customers. Also, there was competition from other long distance telephone companies involved with establishing network-marketing companies that also hindered my growth. People just simply wouldn't remain loyal when they were offered money to switch their service. Thus, this prevented me from getting other people to join because no commission was being made. However, by receiving the checks on a monthly basis, this proved to me that network marketing does work. Whatever, the outcome, I was convinced that telecommunications network marketing is a successful way to get financial independence through leveraging your money and time. But the critical part is that, you need the support of other people who are willing to invest their money, seek challenges, and opportunities as you did to achieve success.

In order to be an independent distributor or to own your own business, you must invest financially, and it was worth the risk. I received checks consisting of bonuses, commissions, and overrides in the mail every day. The best reward is when your find other people seeking these types of marketing opportunities to build an organization and we all become wealthy. Based on this successful experience, I have become a strong fan and advocate of network marketing as a way to get out of debt and to live your dreams.

Building a network marketing organization was fun, but the hardest part was getting people involved in catching the vision (the big picture of financial freedom). Because of my experience in network marketing, I have learned that most people are looking for ways of making some money, but are skeptical and not willing to invest their money and time to earn financial independence through network marketing opportunity because of its past representation. By understanding this pitfall and being a part of a network marketing team, I have learned that people can overcome their failures and realize their dreams. We must realize that there are large markets in the telecommunications and energy industries, and the health and personal care services that are not touched that could afford every American an opportunity to get out of debt through their lucrative network marketing compensation plan. One of the biggest obstacles for American people to overcome is to coming to realize that the American Dream will never come into existence by working a regular job.

To get out of debt, first you must desire to. Then you must start reading books, and magazines pertaining to your interest. I was interested in starting a business in network marketing, so I begin to read *Network Marketing, Newsweek, Business News, Success,* and *Time* magazines to name a few, to learn more and stay current on network marketing technology, the Internet, and the World Wide Web. I also obtained information from the Internal Revenue Service (IRS) that direct sales through network marketing was a good business and a vital way to distribute products and services to the people, and it is not a pyramid (See Chapter 2, "Is Network Marketing an Illegal Pyramid?" Page 57). As technology advances into the 21st Century, we will see that all forms of networks and network-marketing mergers will hit a high because of the Internet. Everything is being operated on the Internet and advertised on the web. We see network wars taking place among Fortune 500 companies and small business companies merging into networks for a share and control of the technology industry. If your company is not on the Internet, you will probably have limited customers or not be in business in the future. This includes businessmen, the general public, and housewives who are using the computer for their personal business transactions on the Internet. The Internet movement consists of personal banking, advertisement, voice and E-mails, e-commerce, water, gas, electric bills, and other transactions via the Internet. Every day we see more technological changes coming into existence and more people getting involved in training and joining some type of network partnership.

Because of the ability to conduct large-scale business on the Internet, there will be very few corporate jobs available other than service-related jobs. The people will have to get involved in the **"Network Generation"**, which is the trend of the future.

America has always been a free enterprise society and only about fifteen to twenty percent of the American people have taken advantage of this system. Under the industrial trend, most Americans have been working a typical job, and this will not create financial independence. The only way to benefit from any economic system in a free enterprise society is through owning a business and investing. Since America is a free enterprise country and with the Internet and wireless society coming into existence, the number of people involved in network marketing will increase. The truth concerning network marketing for those who think it is illegal, wrong, or not for Christians, I got news for you. Network marketing opportunities have been around every since the world has been in existence, and we all have been involved in network marketing whether is has been for our use, someone else's gain to make money, or to obtain support for a service or a cause. **"America the Land of Opportunities,"** supports network marketing opportunities, entrepreneurship and self-employment opportunities, and is based on the creativity principles of God found in the Bible. Network marketing has been used in conducting business with our local, state and federal governments. If you are working on a job and marketing products and services for an individual or company, you are marketing products or services for fulfilling that particular company or individual's vision. If you have ever been involved in a club or organization you have been networking. Where two or three people exchange goods and services for a benefit or for money, it is still called 'networking" or network marketing." It is important that you understand this concept in order to understand the different between legal and illegal network marketing, and not classified all actions of network marketing opportunities as illegal. We have to decide whether we want to get involve in a distribution network opportunity to create a profit or do we want to get involved in a network marketing opportunity for a non-profit organization for a cause and may or may not get paid. Whatever the circumstances, it is up to you to make a decision of your involvement in a network marketing companies when it pertains to a cause or creating wealth to obtain financial freedom to live the American Dream.

I have learned many lessons during my life, and I hope this information will benefit you in making effective choices for your financial life. The key to the American Dream, financial independence and escaping the American job trap, is not working on a job. The focus is to create a business or invest where your money can work for you. The necessary characteristics for operating a business are being goal oriented, having perseverance, and being committed to success. It is very important that you don't give up until you see the vision fulfilled. Thomas Edison, Alexander Graham Bell, and George Washington Carver and the other great inventors, and all they needed was perseverance in order to succeed. There are a lot of if's and quitting in business before any breakthrough, so don't give up. Keep the faith and God will help you. To quit means that you will have to carry out another person's vision. Be a winner, don't quit, and be all you can be since you can only live life once. If you are satisfied with working on a job, this is fine. At least, you know why you don't have financial independence, and how it can be created to change your life.

In summary:

There is a risk aspect attached to every goal. Most people would say a job doesn't have any risk and this is untrue. Individuals never know when they are going to be laid off, have enough money to pay their bills, pass over for a promotion, or able to maintain the high job performance quota to keep their present salary.

When you are buying stocks and mutual funds, you run the risk of yielding an increase on the money you have invested, and being knowledgeable of what company to invest your money. If you are anticipating on getting involved with a network marketing company, the risk is finding a company that will stay in business long enough for a return on your money and finding people with vision that understand the concept of creating money to obtain wealth. Most people are more skeptical about getting involved with network marketing companies as opposed to investing in stock and mutual fund companies, because they perceived it as a greater risk of lost.

Life in itself is a risk and as long as we live, opportunities will come and go. We just have to pray and do our homework and know when to and not to invest in an opportunity and be cautious about risk in all of your investments.

We have listed some special quotations in this book on the next page that will motivate and help you in taking the proper steps in changing your destiny before it is too late. If you don't want to have a better life, think about changing someone's life around you. Read the quotations on pages 44-45 and meditate on them to get out of debt, so you can escape the American job trap and obtain control of your financial future. Everyone was born with a special gift and equal potential to be all they can be in life whether they are a Christian or not. You don't have to be a Christian to know how to create wealth because most Christians do not understand the principle of sowing and reaping from a business point of view to establish wealth for their financial future. The devil has blinded the people's mind and heart to this principle, so he can control their quality time during the day by working on a job for money. Any time you work for something, you become a slave to it and this is why God's principles endorsed creativity and increase by building relationships versus a system of power struggles, control, pride, and greed. The white race controls the majority of the wealth in the government and corporations, and this is the race that has control and power over the labor force. Many times, I have associated a job with being in a prison since you have a person in control over you to watch you and tell you what to do with so many rules to abide by. The most stressful ones are having a certain time to report to work and a certain time to leave work, thirty minutes for lunch, fifteen minutes for breaks (morning and evening), and two-week vacations. The difference between a job and being in prison is that you get to spend weekends and evenings with your family.

It is very important to understand that the America economy is based on a free enterprise system, which allows your money to work for you through investments, which is based on the biblical principles of sowing and reaping (Genesis 1:11-12, Galatians 6:7-8, and Matthew 25:14-30). It also allows you to be your own boss or Chief Executive Officer. As you read other chapters in this book, you will definitely be set free and have a better understanding of how wealth is created to live a prosperous life.

Realistic Quotations to Evaluate Your Life's Situation and Progress

These quotations are designed to motivate you to change and take control of your financial life.

1. **You Don't Get Wealthy by Working for Someone Else's Dream. You Get Wealthy by Making Your Money Work for You.**

2. **You Must Know Alternative Ways to Create Money Besides Working on a Job.**

3. **Network Marketing Opportunity is a "Vision" for Financial Breakthroughs.**

Most people spend their whole life working, but never ever get rich. They buy more, but just get into more debt. They worry about money and their jobs. They want things they can't afford. And sadly to say, they sit and hope for a breakthrough, but never takes advantage of it when it comes.

4. You Must Have a Vision for Your Life or Someone Else Has One Planned for You.

5. The Key To Wealth Is:

   You have to create your own breakthrough to allow
   Your money to work for you.

6. If You Continue to "Think" and "Do" the Things You Have Always Done. Then You Will Continue to Get the Same Results.

   The problem is renewing your mind from a programmatic worldly system to a creative mind; then change what you are doing.

7. You Must Deal With Your Money or Your Money Will Deal With You.

8. The Only Way for Your Situation to Change Is to Do Something Different Than What You Are Always Doing.

9. God Wants You to Dream Your Wisest Dream and Do All You Can to Fulfill It.

10. If You Think You Can, Then You Can. It's a Mind Thing.

CHAPTER 2–A REVOLUTION OF NETWORK OPPORTUNITIES AND UNDERSTANDING THE POWER BEHIND IT

A Network Revolution

A "Network Revolution" has started and it is creating changes in our economic system as never before in history. Business opportunities are surfacing with high profit incentives for people that are eager to take the risk. We are moving out of the industrial age into the technological age. The power behind the movement is deregulation of the telecommunications and utility industries. Everything is moving quickly and before you can learn one system, a new system is invented.

What is the network revolution? To many of the big companies, it is about control. The network revolution is here with high speed, volume, and change. Timing is essential and critical. The revolution is not only affecting the technology industry, but it is affecting everyone. To many families, the network revolution is also about survival since it is causing so many job layoffs. To many families it is the beginning of wealth. The most surprising thing is the movement is unpredictable. We don't know where it will end, and what will be the next service or product that will be invented.

It seems that many people are not in tune with the effect this network revolution will have on them. Are you prepared to make a successful transition to the network revolution? The network movement will not only affect large businesses; it is affecting service provided for and to individuals in their homes and small and home-based businesses. Most of the technology companies are on the competitive edge to create ways for people and businesses to move smoothly into the network movement. Wireless technology is transforming the total world system. The network generation will include new technology consisting of improved electronic equipment; such as wireless telephones, wireless pagers, fiber optics, computers, software packages, fax machines, the Internet, the world wide web, television, satellites, cable, user packages, network and direct marketing. Do you have a fax machine, computer, digital television, pager, or cellular telephone in your office or home? Are you able to communicate with your neighbor by the Internet? If you don't have any of these things, then you have a lot of catching up to do. Since we are moving into the technology age of networks and electronic equipment, it is essential to take advantage of all the networking opportunities. These opportunities and jobs will be in the area of engineers, internet providers, switching service providers, integrated services, computer (technicians, specialists, trainers, programmers), user services, direct and network marketers, contractors, consultants, inventors, etc. All of these occupations will be created in the network generation.

Timing is critical to the network generation. This is why network and/or direct marketing distributors will be essential. It will be quicker and safer to buy your products and services from your friends rather than through a company you don't know or trust. This is because it will not be easy to get background reports concerning the stability of newer companies producing products and services quickly. Therefore, more people will rely on network and/or direct marketing distributors' opinions. Any company, whether network marketing or traditional, may be in business today and gone tomorrow. There is no protection against this from happening. Most network marketing companies will be around because as the products and services change, they trade in their equipment or purchase new equipment at a reduced rate to meet the change. Also, you will get good quality and stable equipment, not the cheap items in inventory. In addition, the new products and services will be moving so fast that people will have to rely on their friends in network marketing or direct sales to ensure they get the best equipment at the most economical price. Companies will charge higher prices for an item until competition occurs. People looking for quality, stability and the best price when purchasing services and products will rely heavily on the recommendations of their friends.

Strategic partnership will also be helpful in starting new businesses and services quickly. The total benefit of the technology and network movement is that you can leverage each other's expertise and strengthen your market's position. The power of leveraging in network/direct marketing will be discussed in this chapter.

If you start today, you and your partners can create the networks of the future from a position of competitive strength. The real challenge is for your team and/or partners to position themselves to provide some form of network service to be included in the "network generation" and be a part of the "gold rush." Any form of networking will generate an unbelievable income in the New Millennium due to leveraging people, time, and resources.

What Is the Power of Network Marketing?

THE "VISION" OF NETWORKING

- **ATTRACTS AND HELPS LARGE NUMBER OF PEOPLE WITH SIMILAR NEEDS**

- **CAUSES YOU TO GET PAID FOR USING THE PRODUCTS AND SERVICES**

- CREATES UNITY AND RELATIONALSHIP BUILDING

- FULFILLS FINANCIAL NEEDS OF MONEY WORK-ING FOR YOU

- CAUSES YOU TO GET PAID FOR YOUR EFFORT AND OTHERS

- LEVERAGES YOUR TIME AND MONEY

- BUILDS TEAMS AND DUPLICATE EFFORTS

- REAPS FINANCIAL REWARDS TOGETHER.

- OFFERS OPPORTUNITY TO OWN YOUR OWN BUSINESS VS. JOBSHIP

- OFFERS OPPORTUNITY TO GET IN LINE WITH GOD BIBLICAL PRINICIPLES

Network Marketing Offers Debt Elimination By Leveraging

What is Leveraging and How Does it Work?

Explanations and Examples of Leveraging

Illustration No. X

1. If you work on a job eight hours a day for five days a week and get paid $200 a week. What would be your weekly paycheck be? $200. Are you leveraging your time and money in this example? No.

2. If you worked as an independent contractor for a company that markets long distance services, the first thing you would do is enroll for $99 and recruit others to purchase the services. Suppose you enroll 10 other people in 5 days. The following week the company will pay you $210 in a commission check for your recruiting and training efforts; plus purchases of services and products. What will you receive at the end of the week a. or b.?

    a. $210 _____

    b. $2,100_____

If you checked b, you are correct. Your paycheck would be $2,100 or more at the end of the week. If each recruit duplicates your effort and time, they would receive a check also for the same amount. When this process is repeated, it is called leveraging.

Example:

$210 Income paid to you.

x 10 No. of recruits on your team.

$2,100 Check received

Suppose the 10 recruits signed up 10 people each that would be 100 people. Then your paycheck for one week would be $21,000 per week. ($210 x 100 = $21,000)—Unbelievable, isn't it. The is the power of network marketing when people are working together to accumulate wealth or income for a special benefit.

Illustration X explains the type of financial impact that network marketing can have on your life, how it works, and how it can help you achieve your goals and dreams. Based on the above illustration, the question now is—Why continue to work on a job for money when you can make more money through establishing a business as a network marketing consultant and distributing various products and services on the internet or through a strategic plan? I know there are many people trying to make ends meet who are barely making it from one day to another. This doesn't have to be, when there are good and approved network marketing companies offering opportunities with good compensation programs and benefits for you to join. These companies are recruiting for individuals like you and me to become a part of their independent contractors or distributors marketing team to distribute their services and products in exchange for commission, residual income, and bonus vs. a fixed salary. With a system like this, you and the company both win. This is known as a **win-win** situation.

NETWORK MARKETING SUPPORTS GETTING PAID FOR USING PRODUCTS AND SERVICES WHEN YOU SHARE THEM WITH OTHERS AND GETTING PAID ON REFERRALS WHEN OTHER PEOPLE JOIN AND PURCHASE PRODUCTS AND SERVICES.

Insight Into The Power of Network Marketing

The telecommunications industry was deregulated in 1982 and in 1999, the utility industry was deregulated. This may have meant absolutely nothing to most people other than lower or higher telecommunications or utility rates. Many people are still unaware of the impact being created by the technological industry in every aspect of our lives including medicine and medical equipment for now and in the future.

On the other hand, many people are being a part of the changes taking place in the world today by the numbers of pagers and cellular phones being used by individuals young and old. As technology advances, we will see more and move innovative equipment and ideas in action paving the way to a wireless society. The growth of technology is global with unbelievable wealth, changes, and surprises. Thus, technology has changed the economic status of many people who desire to be financially independent and to control their lives. To capitalize on the technology movement financially, many people are finding opportunities to become wealthy through selling products and services for various companies seeking independent distributors or contractors.

On the next page, an illustration will be shown of the income

.D

receives as an independent distributor and contractor.

Illustration: Income Received From Network Marketing Distributors

$20.00 Commission from your usage

+ 10.00 Commission from other people's usage

30.00

x200 Number of people in your team.

$6,000 Monthly income received

x 12

$72,000 Yearly income received

Based on this illustration, would you be more interested in getting involved in a network-marketing program as shown above? I am sure you would if the opportunity presented itself. This is the type of opportunity being offered today through network marketing companies. Due to the technological movement, more and more people will get involved in network marketing companies to capitalize on the financial impact of getting paid to use the services versus paying for them. Because of the type of income, one can see why it important to understand and get involved in the network marketing opportunity. This type of income is being realized simply by recruiting and training other people in network ventures as compared to what people are getting paid in salary, working an eight to five job everyday. The money that will be generated from network marketing opportunities is more than the human mind can contain. These types of network opportunities are happening in the telecommunications industry, waste management, health, utility, and by the Internet. Companies are in business because they want people to buy their products and services for a profit. This is one of the major reasons of advertising and recruiting individuals. Under the traditional system, the company will manufacture the products and will provide the services, and then hire a salesman to sell the services to receive a monthly commission check. This is how the salesman is paid. If a company doesn't keep their customers it will probably go out of business. Also, if the salesman doesn't keep his customers, he will not be able to generate monthly income for $500, $10,000–$40,000 a month or more.

Traditional companies are competing with network marketing companies to keep their customers happy by offering them discounts or checks in the mail to keep them from switching services or products. The fact is that an independent contractor can receive commission of $10,000-$40,000 a month or more, plus discounts, bonuses, and residual income based on his effort and the group volume. This is what the traditional companies don't want you to understand, so you will not become involved with network marketing and gain financial independence. As long as ordinary people don't understand the financial impact of getting involved with network marketing opportunities to capitalize on the technology movement, larger corporations will continue to control their time and money and reap all the benefits and rewards. I thank God for network marketing companies because these companies have created opportunities, making it possible for the ordinary person to change their financial life.

I hope this information concerning network-marketing opportunities has contributed to a better understanding of the concept, and how it can change your financial well being. Network marketing opportunity has always been powerful, and it is not new. It started long ago when products and services were exchanged between two or more people. The proof, power, strength, and effectiveness of networking are displaced in organizations, clubs, and large groups of people. Network marketing opportunities have surfaced to get the respect it deserves to be one of the leading investments to the American dream as far as obtaining financial independence. This is all due to the technological movement, which has created a faster pace for getting products and services to the consumer via the Internet by direct sales. This has eliminated the middlemen, wholesalers, warehouses, and has caused many people to lose their jobs in corporate America. My goal is to help people see network marketing opportunities; not as a pyramid, but as a "vision" from God and a way to be blessed in a free enterprise country where opportunities are the backbones of its financial successes. America is the land of the free, brave, and opportunity, not for its name, but because our country's economy is built on capitalism and a nation under God. If a person does not seek opportunities, there is a great possibility that they will never reap the benefits of a capitalist society of becoming financial independence. A job can not produce wealth and it is not designed to do so. A job should be viewed as a temporary means of earning money to get seed money to invest in starting your own business. Many times individuals have worked on a job just to be trained and get the knowledge needed to start their own businesses. The No. 1 goal for anyone working on a job should be to obtain the skill for becoming self-employed to avoid struggling to meet basic everyday needs and to obtain a better position on the job. Minority should really try to be economically empowered since there is so much discrimination on jobs and 97 percent of the Black race depends on government jobs. In the private corporation, jobs are very competitive and very few blacks are hired because most of the jobs are owned by the white majority. If blacks are hired in the jobs, it is usually to have a token person to satisfy the Equal Employment Opportunity (EEO) quota. This is why the EEO policy was established. In the past, minority could only get jobs in the government since it was less prejudice in their hiring practices. Working on a job does not empower anyone, it is just a way for some people to meet their needs temporary.

Competition and Market Share: Statistics To Understanding Network Marketing

There are millions of households in America that could use some types of products or services offered by network marketing companies. About 20-50% of the households in America could be interested in becoming distributors.

Presently, there are more than 100 network marketing companies in existence today in America, and more and more companies are using Independent Contractors to distribute their goods. These companies and distributors are in competition with each other to market the products and services they represent. Individuals distribute most of the products and services from the Internet. Since the Internet is able to reach many people, there will be more households involved in network marketing on a larger scale daily. The Internet will enhance the primary way of marketing, sponsoring, and selling products and services

The economic trend shows more companies originate on the Internet. This changes the way business is being conducted rapidly. Network marketing companies have proven to be the most cost effective way to conduct business producing extraordinary income. More companies are developing network marketing partnerships to help keep the overhead cost low or in some cases eliminate the overhead cost altogether, especially salaries paid to salesman. Distributors for network marketing companies are paid commissions, bonuses, and overrides only if they perform. This is a substantial saving for the company, and it cuts their costs in the advertising department tremendously. This one of the reason more companies are using the network marketing compensation plan to recruit for marketing their services and products.

Most people do network marketing part-time from one to three hours per week. Full-time is about one to three hours four to five times a week. Most network marketing independent contractors retire in 5 years as opposed to 30 years for regular Jobbers. Network marketing is administered through team leveling building, which is called multi-level marketing, which can create a full-time income from a part-time effort. Two great characteristics of Network Marketing are Low Risk and Compensation plan:

Low Risk

1. Most network marketing distributors don't have to worry about going out of business nor have a large overhead debt because there is less money needed for start up and other costs than it takes to start a traditional small business or public franchise.
2. The network marketing company handles the accounting and bookkeeping
3. Most distributors work out of their home.
4. It has low start-up fee usually runs from $10 to $1,000.
5. It has a limited staff, secretary, marketing consulting, accountant, and lawyers.

Compensation

People involved in network marketing usually are paid by a compensation plan for their work and performance efforts. This compensation varies according to the company with whom you have invested in their products or services. Usually if you don't perform you don't get paid. Without understanding the concept and negative publicity, some people rather work on a job because they are sure of earning a salary to pay their bills even if it is just enough to make ends meet. However, for those people working on a job, network marketing allows them to build a business at the same time they are working. Network marketing is a systematic approach or process to get your money to work for you. One of the biggest problems in network marketing is getting or recruiting people to see the vision of building a team to create wealth. Network marketing is a people's business; you need a large quantity of people to join in a limited time to reap the rewards. Network marketing is at its highest level when you have a product or service that will benefit a large number of people. Companies know that people recommending products and services to each other are one of the most credible marketing tools since the Bible and is still effective in growing businesses.

Working For A Company To Distribute Their Products And Services Through Network Marketing

When you are working for a network marketing company, the company pays you commission. The company also offers residual income that you receive over and over again based on the total organization's monthly performance. Residual income is one of the greatest incentives network-marketing companies have to offer a person. It is the type of income that works for you while you are asleep, traveling, or enjoying yourself. Network marketing companies are now offering better compensation plan, free web site, paid vacations as a bonus, cars, tickets to special performances, and a share of the company's total profit once you reach a certain level. When you work for self you have the opportunity to make your own rules such as hours of work and vacation time. Most of all having a business afford you to arrange your schedule to be able to take care of your personal business and children doing the day. To me this is called "living life."

Is Network Marketing an Illegal Pyramid?

The answer to that question is simple; it is a legal business. Network marketing is a financial opportunity offered by companies to individuals to distribute their products and services as an independent contractor. To get involved, the individual must pay a small investment. However, like anything else you have to be cautious of what company you invest your money. The devil wants you to think that network-marketing opportunity is an illegal pyramid to keep people poor, in bondage, and to control their financial well being. This is surely not what the Lord has planned for your life. Network marketing opportunity is confirmed by every word in the Bible, see "Breaking the Financial Curse of Poverty

Over Your Life Through Entrepreneurship: A Divine Calling From God and the American Dream," co-authored by Dr. Betty Lancaster-Short of Howard University and myself. Based on this book, a business in network marketing offers six important things:

a. An opportunity to "visionalize" your financial future.
b. An opportunity for your money to work for you.
c. An opportunity to receive extraordinary income.
d. An opportunity for the ordinary person to be debt free.
e. An opportunity to finance God's kingdom on earth.
f. An opportunity to work less hours, years, and to control your time and destiny.

This book will also eliminate negative and old mindsets, so people can take advantage of every opportunity to live a better and abundant life. Every job with one head chairman at the top and an organization below is a pyramid. If you work for the Federal Government, you work for a pyramid; this is true of a state government or any other corporation that has a leader. A network marketing organization structure is no different, and it serves the same purpose as a franchise or stock opportunity. The Internal Revenue Services (IRS) and the Federal and state governments have approved network marketing opportunity. The person should first check to make sure that the company they are involved with is not operating as an illegal pyramid. There is a checklist on page 61 for steps on evaluating a network marketing company. To find out if a company is operating a legal or an illegal pyramid can be determined by a company's compensation plan. If the company's compensation plan shows an exchange of money only without a product or service being offered, the company is operating as an illegal pyramid. For additional information, see pages 160-161 or call the Better Business Bureau.

Network marketing opportunity is an approved small or home-based business that doesn't put any demands upon a person. You are your own Chief Executive Officer and are in control of your own life. It is a "mini" or private franchise where the most impoverished individuals can be helped to achieved the American Dream.

If network marketing opportunity is not for you, then this is fine. There are other small businesses or ventures that you might want to pursue to obtain wealth. However, I believe God wants Christians to live a debt free and prosperous life through a system of creativity and tithing based on His word.

By becoming an independent distributor or contractor, causes a person to be in a position of ownership to control and lead. In addition, it causes your money to work for you. There are far too many Christians unaware of this principle and are laboring for money daily to survive with no vision to create money for their financial future. Slavery ended when God led the people out of Egypt. A person can pay their tithes and offering, but never get wealth because everything received from God is through an act of Faith. This means that you must do something in the physical realm to activate your faith, which is finding network companies and getting others to join or create a business. The scripture states, "Remember it is the Lord our God who gives you power to get wealth so that His covenant can be established on this earth," Deuteronomy 8:18. This is one of the scriptures in the Bible that supports why I say wealth is created, and not gained by working on a job. There are many people who *need* to change their lives, and want to change their lives by taking immediate action, but network-marketing opportunities seem **not** to appeal to the average masses, ordinary people including Christians; but only to the professional career-minded people. There are a lot of people in need; and this will always be the case because a lot of people are always looking for something free, an easy way out, apprehensive about starting a business or an excuse not to change. In some instances, we find many people that just want to blame others for their life conditions. Some people like the situation of working on a job because they feel secure; and it takes less effort, money, and time than to start a business. These individuals like to fall into the flow of something that is already in existence whether the influence is positive or negative where very little effort is exerted. This is what has happened to 80 percent of the American people including college graduates too.

Based on the existing labor system in place for the American workers, many people have adept and allow the worldly system to control their financial well being by falling into a career pattern already designed for them to live a mediocre or poor life. Being a part of the American labor force has created the "Lazy Man Syndrome," meaning that the workers' have to put little or no energy and effort forth to do the job. The workers operate their jobs similar to robots in which everyone is programmed to perform their job automatically. The work is routine and untouchable, meaning that it can't be changed, and every thing on how to handle a situation is written in a regulation. If you try to change it, someone will reply, "sir, we have done it this way all of our lives, check the regulation." In addition, the mind of workers is not used for creativity and workers find themselves in a catch it 22 situation all their life until retirement unless their jobs are downsized, reengineered, or abolished before they retire. The person who falls into this syndrome system, pays a higher price for life versus a person who takes control of his destiny and creates his own life through the talent and gifts given to him by God.

A business opportunity in Network Marketing is wise, approved, stable, and being taught in almost all colleges today including major Universities. Network marketing opportunity in conjunction with the Internet will be the number one way companies will distribute their products and services to the consumers in the New Millennium. We already have Internet companies such as Amazon, Yahoo, web-hosting and design companies, car dealers, malls, etc. involved in some aspects of network marketing and direct sell ventures. Larger health companies, telecommunications industries, and utility companies are using network marketing independent distributors and contractors. We welcome this opportunity because it pays people well for their efforts versus working on a job for money.

Published in, "The Wall Street Journal Marketplace," Friday, June 23, 1995, "Visions of Wealth and Independence Lead Professionals to Try Multilevel Marketing," Peter L. Hirsen did the unthinkable a few years back: He left a six-figure salary at Cravath, Swaine & Moore, a New York law firm where he was an associate, to become a salesman in the controversial world of multilevel marketing. This is because professionals are seeking more money to have quality time to spend with self and family. By making this change in his life, Mr. Hirsen, who is 29 years old, makes as much as $50,000 a month, mostly in commissions and on down line sales.

There are over 4.1 million people involved in multilevel marketing and it is still growing. Network marketing appeals to all levels of people, especially the would-be business owners who dream of owning a McDonald franchise, Weight Loss Company, or a Christian Television Station, clothing store but don't have the money to invest. Now, most of these people are investing in a "people franchise," which is another name for network marketing opportunity. We find other people seeking ways to invest their money to help other people. These individuals long for the sense of community and belonging that network marketing opportunity often can provide. Some people who get involved with network marketing view it as a way to help women, job rejects, Christians, and many with creative ability in the low-to-middle class neighborhoods who are looking for a way to escape the fruitless life of becoming part of the American labor force network.

The Utility Forecaster, described network marketing as, "basically the 1849 Gold Rush's principles all over again, "The smart way to grow rich." Various others magazines–*Entrepreneurs*, *Success*, *Business Week*, *Black Enterprise*, and *Networking* are always printing success articles telling stories of people who have started their own home-based network business. I believe network marketing can afford all of us the opportunity to have a success story in our lives, and live the American Dream and escape the job trap.

Steps in Selecting a Network Marketing Company

Ask yourself these questions before you invest your money.

1. Can you and other use the products or services being offered?

2. Are the products and services of good quality, right price range, and reliable to use?

3. Does the company offer training to support the distributors and independent contractors?

4. Can you make a profit from the sale of the product or service?

5. Does the company provide a good compensation plan to pay you up front for your efforts?

6. Is the Product and service consumable or what the people can use? Has the product been on the market for a long time?

7. Does the startup fee range from $9.99 through $5,000?

8. How many levels of earned bonuses and commissions are offered?

9. Is this a good reputable company and guarantee customer's satisfaction?

10. Do you have to be concerned about keeping inventory on hand?

11. Do you have to collect money from your customers?

12. Is there a renewal fee? How much?

13. How long has the company been in business? Does it have a public image?

14. How difficult is it to advance to various levels?

15. How often and when do you get paid?

16. Can you market the product/service on the Internet?

17. What is the risk involved?

18. What is the risk of the company going out of business or able to pay commission?

These questions are to be used as a checklist to help eliminate the risk of getting involved with an unsound network marketing company. Be cautious of obtaining large inventory up front.

Eighteen Steps To Be Successful in Network Marketing

1. Always take steps and time to train yourself.

2. Read books, magazines, newspaper, direct mail, etc.

3. Attend your Chamber of Commerce's seminars given for Small Businesses.

4. Attend other related meeting, briefing, etc.

5. Go to conventions.

6. Do conference calls.

7. Sponsor and attend luncheons or banquets.

8. Get involved with other network companies and programs.

9. Stand Steadfast. Never quit.

10. Develop a strategic plan.

11. Teach others to see the power behind networking.

12. Never quit believing in your vision and self.

13. Always be coachable and teachable.

14. Understand the need to share information as a marketing technique vs. selling.

15. Never depend or wait for your up-line to grow your business.

16. Be a great team player. Find out what you need to do, and do your part well.

17. Figure your earning based on the company's compensation plan. Know and understand how you are to make money.

18. Always check on the company's rating before signing up. Be led by your spirit.

The Rewards of Network Marketing

The common and ordinary people are able to live the
American Dream

- Leveraging your time and money is the key–The system is duplicable

- High Finances—High revenue can be obtained through strategic planning

- Teaming–Working together for strength and building an organization

- Debt Freedom–No longer living from pay check-to-check

- Residual Income–Your money continues to work for you even when you're sleeping

- Set Hours of work–No more 2-4 hours a day.

- Be home with children–Enjoy family life and see children growing up

- More time–Time to pursue your dreams

- Money works for you–Don't have to work for money on a job

- Unlimited income–Never live on a fixed income any more

- Able to make a financial contribute to charity–Support others in need

- More time with God–Have time to feed your spiritual man.

These are some of the major rewards that are associated with a network marketing opportunity. Does working on a job offer the same types of rewards? The answer is no. Maybe for those people in top management.

Benefits of Becoming a Consultant Agent, Independent Contractor, or Distributor Through Network Marketing

- Creates an Opportunity to Own a Business–Able to share your talent and gifts

RD

- Helps Others to Own a Business–Build Unity and Teams to support each other

- Permanent Income–No temporary income working from pay check to pay check

- Paid on Group Volume Income vs. One Income–Team building and leveraging

- An Employer vs. an Employee–Work to fulfill your own dream on earth

- Received Unlimited Income–Revenue being produced continuously

- Open Door for Money to Work for you–Allow money to circulate and multiply

- Low Investment–Startup cost to own a business is less than $1,000

- Tax Write-off–Able to receive tax benefits and deductions from owning a business

- Control Own Time–Freedom to choose what you do and how to use on time

- Leveraging Opportunity—Benefit to obtain wealth through duplication

These benefits are offered to the independent contractors or distributors and these benefits are only partakers by only 20 percent of the American population or less. The other 80 percent of the American population are workers and receive salary, job promotion, and pay more taxes and have less deduction.

Empowering Men and Women in Network Marketing

Who are these people?

- Overworked and underpaid?

- Christians who want to spend more time in their ministry

- Work on two jobs

- Not enough money to live day-to-day

- No control over time

- Long work hours

- Living from pay check to pay check

- Routine days

- Bad credit, no credit or bankruptcy record

- Same amount of money received day-after-day

- Looking for a job or to change job

- Not able to use your creative ability on your job

If you feel you are affected by at least eight out of the twelve above needs and desires, then you have vision. Now you must find a network marketing company to invest in the business. Read this book and it will help you to minimize your risk. If you are getting the same results over and over again after many years of working on a job, then you need to analyze other ways of making money to financially support your life. There is not going to be a change by having only a job or working two jobs. Remember the principle of insanity is to do the same thing over and over again and expect a different result.

Most traditional jobs only afford the average people an opportunity to barely live and create liabilities. This is because they are working for money. The American Dream is never intended for you to work for someone else in a capitalistic society. This is one of the reasons people are barely making it and are living from paycheck to paycheck. There is an old saying that if you continue to do the same thing you will continue to get what you have always gotten, the same result.

If this is what has been happening to you, then you must be ready to make some changes. To make a change is to pursue opportunities other than working on a job to have a better financial life.

Ten Steps to Generating Wealth

How Are The Doors Of Business Opportunities Opened To Change Your Financial Situation?

- By owning a business (small or home based) for yourself

- Investing money in the Stock Market

- Finding ways to invest your money so it can work for you

- Investing in mutual funds

- Investing in Real Estates

- Getting involved with a Network Marketing Company

- Creating a new invention (a service, product, and dot.com company)

- Writing books, poems and plays

- Taking advantage of tax deductions by becoming self-employed

- Purchasing a franchise (Private or Public)

- Engaging in sport activities, music, dancing, arts and crafts

- Being a professional doctor or lawyers

- Becoming a consulting or independent contractor or distributor.

The above list shows some of the ways of generating wealth for your life. Notice I didn't say put your money in a bank, because you only need to keep enough money in a bank in case of an emergency. Most people think that all you do with money is to work for it, spent, or save it, and this is not true. The best thing for most people to do is to sit down with a financial planner, so they can share ways to put their money into a market that will work for them. The reason for the financial planner is to help you budget and find a place to invest your money. Money must circulate and not stand still to be accumulated. If you have money in the bank, the bank is circulating your money by investing in stocks and bonds and loaning your money to others in return for interest. This is called using "Other Peoples Money, (OPM)." The banks are becoming richer and wealthier while they use your money and charge you interest to use and maintain it. This is why you must find ways to invest your money in order to generate income for yourself, and put a minimum amount of your money in the bank for savings for emergency funds. If you want to invest in a network marketing opportunity, check with your friends or look on the Internet. If you find a company you are interested in, call the Better Business Bureau to check out the company's profile.

The Biggest Fear/Concern of the American Worker Today Is Job Security

Network marketing business is becoming the fastest growing and most rewarding way to make a living in the future versus the traditional job due to the technological age.

Companies sell their products or services through network marketing because it reduces time, the need for up-front advertising and marketing expenses of getting products and services to the end consumer.

Normally, there is a small start-up or investment cost and fewer employees are required, than as in the traditional companies. The small start-up costs give people the opportunity to own their own business instead of working on a job for someone else. In the traditional business, there is only one person at the top, the President or the Chief Executive Officer (CEO), in which mostly likely you will never achieve in a lifetime. Most people working in a traditional pyramid never get to the top because of their grade levels. They are also hindered by the other network systems in place such as the Good Old Boys' and Girls' Networks and special society clubs, and they choose who should be at the top.

Under the traditional system of a job, most people file a W2 tax form and pay income tax several times. When you own your own business, the person files a 1099's tax form and receive a tax deduction. Based on American history, during the colonial days, most people worked in their homes and were their own CEO. It was during the industrial age when this trend shifted and more people started working outside their homes. People were forced to work long hours and in many cases longer than five days a week with minimum wages, (see the movie Norma Rae). The industrial age created the labor movement, and labor unions were developed to have a voice for the concerns of the workers. People working on assembly lines were treated as slaves.

Now, the economic trend of today is technology, paving the way to a wireless society. It is so powerful and has created shorter working hours with wealth, along with an explosion of home-based businesses, which has changed the way business is being conducted worldwide. It is a movement of "information" and it is so fast, electronic driven and referred to as the "super information Highway." Due to the electronic advancement, networking as a way to distribute products and services is a form of marketing that will once again put people back into their homes to work. Being able to network and operate a business in the homes by computers through the Internet has changed people's lives spiritually, financially, physically, and mentally.

The technological age has opened many doors to the average person to be prosperous economically. Whereas under the job system, instead of helping people to get financial independence, most people found that they worked harder or have to work two jobs and still didn't earn enough income to pay their debts or make ends meet. A person working two jobs to obtain additional money is a "no," "no," since the second job could place them in another tax bracket. This could result in a higher incremental rate, which means that when individuals files their income taxes for the calendar year; instead of getting a refunds, they would owe more taxes. A second job creates higher taxes and less tax deductions; and therefore, there is no gain for your efforts. A person with a business receives tax deductions, and this is the reason why some people get involve with a business. If your financial needs are not being met by working one job, then why do you think your needs can be met by working a second job. To help a person offset its debts, see ways of creating wealth on pages 68 and 69. Most people might not have the mindset to start a traditional business, but most people can get involved with a network marketing business opportunity. It is a team's approach with little or no college education.

It is time that more people move into the economic stream of ownership and/or self-employment, because the present economic system has created a lot of liability for the American middle-class labor force. Some of the problems created by the present working system are:

1. Higher ratio of debts due to a fixed income earned by receiving wages, which do not provide a person with enough money to pay the monthly bills.

2. An environment where mothers have to leave their homes to work on jobs away from their children during the prime time of their children's lives.

3. A major draw back is that the job's system causes people to be on welfare if they can not qualify for a job. No jobs, no money. The next thing is public assistance.

4. Everyone does not qualify for a job and many minorities are turned down for the best and idea jobs, or the jobs that pay more money. This creates a problem and causes a rise in drugs, crimes, and poverty in communities.

The potential to get people off welfare to permanent jobs by our Government has created an opportunity for more impoverished families to become part of the labor force. However, this does not solve the problem, but shifts the problem. The main interest of the Government is to balance the budget and reduce the number of welfare recipients, but the "struggle to pay debts and live a better life by having enough money to pay all monthly debts, still exist for 80 percent of the American people." This is why is it up to the individuals to understand why they are in debt and how to get out of debt. Let us review the average American spending pattern, and we will show you why people are in debt, how to get out of debt, and a checklist of opportunities to get out of debt (see budgets) on pages 95-100.

I use all the wealth building programs to create wealth; but of all the ways, the simplest way to get out of debt is through network marketing company. Most of the companies do not require a person to have a degree, attend college, or have any special training or skills. It does not discriminate against sex, race, religion, economic status, and disabled or handicapped people. It enables all people with a strong desire to change their financial well being to do so. Network marketing has been reported to have these characteristics:

- It is the fastest growing and number one income maker of six-digit figures.

- Network marketing has produced most millionaires.

- It offers an opportunity for all people to get wealthy.

- It is not a pyramid scheme: the IRS recognizes it.

- It is a "vision" in line with God's biblical plan to create wealth.

Types of Marketing Programs

Various types of marketing programs to distribute goods and services to consumers are:
- Door-to-Door

- Catalog sales

- Direct Sales

- Direct Marketing

- Telephone Sales

- Network Marketing

- Multi-level marketing

- Retail Stores

- Wholesale stores

- Manufacturing Stores

- Distribution Stores

- Internet Sales

- Radio sales

- Word of Mouth

- Cold Calling

- Warm Market

- Relationship Marketing

- Fax Machines

- Franchising

- Vendor Machines

- Home Deliveries

- Discount Stores (B.J. and Sam)

- Department Stores

Most of the above types of marketing programs are traditional methods of marketing. The newer and most productive ways of marketing are through the Internet, vending machines, franchising, multi-level marketing, direct/network marketing, and word-of-mouth sales.

Finding the Right Business to Do in the New Millennium

We are living in a time when our society is adopting a totally new way of doing business in the corporate world. Some may call this the automation age, the technology age, the computer age, the information age, or the electronic age. Whatever it may be called, it is here today and it has changed the way we conduct business, how we think, and what we do. In this book, we have chosen to use any of the above terms to express the movement of the New Millennium Age.

For people who want to escape being in the 80 percent of Jobbers, network marketing opportunity is the right business at the right time to be self-employed in order to capitalize on the technological movement of the 21st Century. The technology revolution is the driving and controlling force affecting the total well being of people's lives financially and socio-economically. We are forced into this movement whether we are ready for it or not. As in all movements, we must ensure that we take the necessary actions to participate and capitalize on it early to reap the financial benefits quickly or someone else will. We must read and take classes that will mold our lives to help us to move smoothly into the new century. The technology movement is fast, quick, and extraordinarily rewarding economically and financially. Like all new beginnings, we have an opportunity to be successful by taking responsibility today. This movement will definitely affect our lives whether we choose to do something now or stay where we are. The days of working for someone else are changing. We are moving back to home-based businesses, small businesses, as cited in Faith Popcorn's book, "The Popcorn Report."

In the large corporate offices, companies are forming strategic alliance networks they can leverage whenever a choice market place opportunity arises as cited in John Conlon and Melissa Giovagnoli's book, "The Power of Two."

On a small corporate scale, home-based businesses are booming and are being formed in great numbers. These home-based businesses are very powerful and some are forming strategic alliances through network marketing as distributors or independent contractors. They can capitalize on the great technology movement by getting services and products closer and faster to the consumers by leveraging. Leveraging is the key word for accumulating wealth, and it will determine the amount of money in your pocket. Applied knowledge and information are second to leveraging. Finally, how well we are able to team or partner with others will determine our personal economic stability and status for the future. More and more people are catching this vision and are leveraging and establishing strategic alliance networks by coming together and sharing knowledge and experience. If the American dream is to come to pass, now is the time.

It is stated that over 30,000 new businesses are being born daily by using other people's money. The knowledge behind using other people's money is to have some money to invest and start your own business to allow your money to work for you. This is the secret behind how money is created. This is a new concept along with a new movement, new time, and new thinking. If you think you can get involved with the movement without any money, then you have missed the vision. For so many years, the people have missed the mark of having abundance by working for others to get money, and not pursuing their own vision to achieve their desires in life.

Does Network Marketing Work for All?

Most of the people might say I have tried multi-level marketing and it doesn't work for me.

The Reasons why it has not worked are:

1.   No Vision—No clearly defined purpose

2.   No decision–Not enough information to make a choice

3.   Negative concept concerning network marketing

4.   Fees to join—Skeptical about paying the money to go into business. Not understanding using other people's money nor the importance of investing your money to create money

5.   Not seeing network marketing as a legal business, but as a pyramid

6.   Seeing network marketing as selling vs. sharing knowledge

7.   Unable to recruit people including friends and families

8.   People not maintaining loyalty.

9.   No steadfastness or endurance

10. No leadership up-line

11. No strategic Plan or goal in effect for your life

12. Unwilling to change

13. Looking for someone to lead them

14. Not able to recruit people

15. No belief that it will work

16. Not understanding the concept of how wealth is created

17. Fear of taking risk.

18. Not fully persuaded in their mind

If you have tried networking marketing or another business and it has not worked, review the checklist below. Then reevaluate your situations and try again.

Seventeen Important Things Successful People Have in Common

1. They have a strong desire to succeed.
2. They have a willingness to change.
3. They have a vision and plan to execute.
4. They are part of a team and are able to network and share common goals.
5. They know how to access and use other people's money.

6.   They have mentors to advise them.

7.   They are able to make decisions and act quickly in faith and believe in God and themselves.

8.   They know how to dress for success.

9.   They are self-motivated and goal-oriented.

10. They have a strong desire to possess, achieve, control, and conquer.

11. Their motive or goal is to help or change a situation, to make a difference in the world or in somebody's life.

12. They don't settle for second best: They strive for the best.

13. They understand the concept of creating wealth.

14. They are people with leadership ability and with ambition.

15. They possess character, motivation, competency, courage, perseverance, persistence, determination, influence, and high self-esteem.

16. They never quit seeking opportunities to make things better for themselves and others in life.

17. Overlook the door of failure to get to the door of success.

CHAPTER 3–
FINANCIALLY SUCCESSFUL

What Is Financial Success to You?

1. Financial success means—being in control of your money and time.

2. Financial success means—not worrying where the next penny will come from.

3. Financial success means—not having to depend upon a paycheck.

4. Financial success means—not working on a job.

5. Financial success means—not working nine to five.

6. Financial success means—living in God's abundance and perfect will for my life.

7. Financial success means—having enough to share with others.

8. Financial success means–having to achieve your long-term financial goals.

9. Financial success means–enjoying life without having to worry about your finances.

If what financial success means to you is not included here, list them:

- _____

-

- _____

-

- _____

-

-

- _____

-

Where and How To Invest Your Money?

Understanding about investments and where to put your money to work for you.

Investments are listed according to highest risk by categories.
High Risk
A. Category I—Commodities

Options, Commodities—include such things as beef, soybeans, orange juice, wheat, or products that people might consume.
Why is it High Risk?

A person is speculating that the price of the specific commodity will rise or fall. Institutional traders control the commodity markets.

Moderate Risk
B. Category II—Investments

Stocks

Common stocks represent ownership (equity) in large corporations. Common shares of stocks are traded on New York Stock Exchange, American Stock Exchange, or Over-the-Counter Market. Investors buy stocks to receive dividends. Common stock can be very profitable if bought and sold at the right time. For various stocks, bonds, mutual funds and other investments and how to buy read "Personal Budget Planner" by Eric P. Gelb.

Bonds

Corporate bonds are used by companies to borrow money from investors and promise to return the money with both principal and interest. Investors buy bonds to receive interest income, and capital gains if the bonds are sold before maturity. When market interest rates fall, the price of a bond rises. Conversely, when market interest rates rise, the price of a bond falls. The various types of bonds are High-Yield (Junk) Bonds, state and local bonds, (general obligation bonds, revenue bonds), government bonds, and corporate bonds.

Real Estate

One of the best investment people can make in life in real estate is to own their home. Money is made from real estate if the cash flow from rents exceeds the expenses, and the property is priced fairly. Some forms of real estate investment that people get involve with are time shares, vacation homes, real estate investment trusts, and purchasing homes and reselling them at higher prices. Today, the interest is partnering to buy property.

Mutual Funds

The Myth of Mutual Funds

Many people think that investing their money in mutual funds yields the best return on their investment. However, buyers need to be aware and consider two things:

- When the tax rates are high, the return on your investment could erode.

- When tax rates are high and you die, your wealth could be depleted by estate taxes and other probate costs.

- When buying mutual funds, you should understand the difference between "No-Loads" and "Load" funds.

  - No-Load funds do not charge a fee when you buy shares of a fund.

  - A Load fund charges a fee when you buy shares of the fund.

Low Risk
C. Category III—Savings
Certificate of Deposits (CD)–are generally offered by financial institutions that issue them and can be a good investment when interest rates are high or investors seek a stated rate of return. Always look for a financial institution that is insured by the Federal Deposit Insurance Corporation (FDIC)

Money Markets (MM)—Put your money to work for you in a money market funds.

Banks—are usually financial lending institutions that are authorized to handle your money.

Credit Unions (CU)–Are lending institutions usually operated by membership only

EE Bonds–Are U.S saving bonds that you purchase on the jobs or at banks. They generally grow slowly over a period of time.

Life Insurance—People invest into insurance for protection in case of disability or death. There are various insurance policies to fit individual needs. People often receive dividends and sometimes are able to cash-in the policy once it matures.

High to Low Risk

D. Category IV–Investing in a Company's Advertising and Marketing Programs–as an Independent Contractor or Distributor through Network Marketing Opportunities

Investing in Network Marketing Businesses

Revenue created through network marketing companies offer individuals an opportunity as owners to leverage investment into the company's advertising and marketing programs by building a network of distributors and independent contractors as owner and buyers. Thus, the company offsets the individual's investment with bonuses, commissions, and residual income.

Speculation depends upon a company building a team of investors consisting of pooling 3-5 distributors or independent contractors to a team based on a matrix system. Each team is designed to reproduce distributors or independent contractors to build a marketing network of users. The company's purpose is to create a network of distributors or independent contractors to market their products or services versus hiring salesmen. This is one way a company can ensure a demand of buyers for the services or products being created or manufactured at a more economical cost. When an individual does not understand this concept, the involvement in network marketing is a high risk. When the individuals understand this concept, the risk is low because more people are involved. It takes a one-time investment fee to become a distributor or independent contractor, but the company may require that the individual buy or use a certain amount of products or services to qualify for commission each month. The greater the number of people involved in the network; the more products or services used; and the higher the commission received. A person is also paid on the group or team volume effort that was produced for that month. Some people are involved in network marketing companies because these companies produce some of the best products and services, and these items can only be bought through a distributor or independent contractor. Many companies reward their distributors and independent contractors with great incentives and benefits such as cars, bonuses based on a percentage of the overall profit of a company, luscious vacations, health and dental insurance, free Internet services, etc. After being in the company and receiving commission, you can deduct the cost of purchasing your services and products from your check and still have unlimited money.

To find individuals interested in starting a network marketing business, look for people who want to invest their money and who can use that company's product or service a lot. Then the risk is low to none when building a team of network marketing investors. Network marketing organization built of distributors or Independent contractors can be powerful when the power of duplication kicks in. Before people get involve in network marketing, they must be able to perceive and understand the power behind networking, obtaining, and keeping customers. Networking simply means (Group + Investors + Teaming + Action) = Monetary Awards. People coming together in oneness to achieve the same common purpose produce numbers in unity and strength with power to influence. Networking plays a must needed part in our finances or in life, generally because the world is set up where we must depend on each other for survival. This is a true statement because whatever we do is depending on fulfilling a need for someone else. Meeting needs of others are the main concepts behind network marketing, which constitutes building relationships by teaming people and resources.

Investments Recommended

a. Stocks–Buy companies that participate in Dividend Reinvestment Programs
    -Reason: Don't have to pay fees or commission to a stock broker.
b. Commercial properties–Invest in properties and sell the property at a higher value than purchased price.
c. Network marketing opportunities–Consist of individuals with a common need working together to achieve a common goal.

When you own a business, you can own stocks. If you get involve with a network marketing company, usually the company will offer you an opportunity to buy the stock.

If you buy commercial properties, you become a landlord instead of a tenant.

Since everyone is different, each person must find the program to put its money in to fit its own situation. However, it is most important for you to find a system that will create the most wealth for you. You can be involved with all types of investments.

Putting some of your money into a bank and spreading it among other banks are great sources to put your money, for savings, but you should not put all of your money into a saving account. The rationale is that the banks give you a very low interest rate on the return of the dollar value. Every person should have some funds set aside in a saving account or in the bank for emergency purposes and for business transactions, but not as a place to invest your money for growth. The banks use your money and other people's money to invest into commercial real estate and other sources for their own advantage and benefit. You never get any dividends or return on the bank's transaction. This is one reason why banks are so wealthy, because they use other people money to invest and create wealth for themselves. The banking idea started by an individual with a vision to create wealth based on fulfilling a need, as a way to help people with their business transactions; and in return, the banks have benefited greatly.

Instead of the banks investing your money, find other sources that you can invest your money and receives a higher return on it, such as mutual funds or 401-K plans. The purpose of the above information is to help you to understand opportunities to invest your money and the value and source of money, and how your money can work for you to create wealth. Don't shy away from investing your money; it has a risk, but so does a job. Of course, people do invest their money in CD's and bonds from the banks, but you get a lower interest rate of return, than if you put your money in some of the other sources as listed on the previous page.

With time and moderate risk, you can generally get a higher rate of return on your investment in property and other business ventures. Whether you receive a high or low return on your business, people should put some money in the bank for emergency and routine savings. Then put some of your money in mutual funds, Keogh, SEP, self-retirement plan for those who own a business, 401-K plan, and then invest in stocks from companies such as AT&T, America on line, etc. Check with a financial advisor or planner to help you find or recommend other investment sources. Also, some family members are very knowledgeable in this area of investment, and libraries have books for you to read on this subject or TelComNet, see information at the end of book.

Steps in How to Make Money to Control Your Financial Future

1. Understand the power behind Investments.

Being able to invest your money where it can work for you is the power source behind accumulating wealth and making money.

2. Know and understand, which major economic systems are governing your money whether it is communism, socialism, or capitalism.

To understand the major economic systems, each one is defined below:

- Communism is a social system marked by the common ownership of the means of production and common sharing of labor and products. It is a system of government, in which the state controls the means of production and a single, usually a authoritarian party, holds power with the intention of establishing a social order; in which, all goods are shared equally as in Cuba and formally, the Soviet Union.

- Socialism is an economic system in which the producers possess political power and the means of producing and distributing goods. A proletariat (a group of people running the system) usually carries out the theory or practice as in England and Italy.

- Capitalism is an economic system marked by open competition in a free market, in which the means of production and distribution are privately or corporately owned. The development is proportionate to increasing accumulations and reinvestment of profits as in the United States and Australia.

If you understand these systems, it will help you in understanding the political structure, forces, and controlling power in place in your country as to what you can do and can't do financially in creating wealth. However, there is no pure system because of the country's governing power of control, which is usually the political influence. The political power in America is the Federal Government, which is a strong network called " bureaucrats" to govern and put control on your finances and regulate your life. These networks consist of governing bodies such as Internal Revenue Service (IRS), The Federal Trade Commission, Interstate Commerce Commission, legislative bodies, judiciary bodies, and partisan on Capital Hill, large corporations, and nonprofit interest groups. All these groups affect your financial life. The IRS is required to approve the business for operation, and the state regulators will give you guideline of what is allowed, the type, and where to conduct the business in your city or state. Also the government will make sure that you pay taxes and are license to operate your business.

3. **You must take the initiative to have a vision, purpose, and plan for your life.**

If you don't have a vision or plan for your financial life, the state or local governing body has a plan for you. It is either a job or welfare.

4. Set up your goals and take action to accomplish them.

People can tell you what you need to do to get out of debt, but it is up to you to implement or execute your dreams and to live them. All good dreams or visions should be to support a need on earth. Therefore, if the desire is in you strong enough, it will come to pass. Every thing in life that we see or use has been made possible through a person's dream or vision such as George Washington Carver, Bill Gates, the Wright Brothers, Oprah Winfrey's show, TransCon Wireless, Inc., AT&T, Mary Kay, Shaklees and Amway products, architects who have designed buildings, the Cancer Society Group, Youth for Life, Families United for Restoration, books written by people, and the list continues. The next person can be you; keep encouraged.

5. Then write your dream/vision in a business plan.

This is called a blueprint of your goals. Every plan will have a mission to be accomplished. The plan or a road map is important because it will show how to begin and complete your vision. This is a feature or guideline for tracking, measuring, and controlling your action as you go forth to achieve your goals. Have you ever put a puzzle together? Well, when you bought it, all pieces of the puzzle were in the box, and you had to put the pieces together. To help you put the pieces together, you have a picture of the completed puzzle on the box. The business plan is a complete designed of your completed "vision" of a product or service.

6. Look for someone to fund your business.

This can be hard if you or your family don't have the money to help fund your venture. Then you should take your business plan to people that you feel might loan you the money. There are capital ventures, angel networks, individuals, and some grants available to help you to get started with your plan. Some people use their credit cards, but buyers should be aware of the financial bondage it can get you in. If you use your credit cards be sure that you will produce enough services or products to pay the card off quickly because of the high interest rate. Most of your monthly payment goes for interest and you have very little money applied toward the principle. This is why it is easier to get credit cards from any company, and this is how credit card can get you in debt. Once you get in debt, bankruptcy is not the best way to get out because the record remains with your credit file as long as you live.

7. Build your network team.

Your network team will consist of your staff, associates, partners, community, government officials (local and state representatives), and other corporations.

8. Finally, implement your plan in action.

This is the time to reward yourself for achieving your goals and objectives for mankind.

Usually, you will reap the financial benefits that come with the package money is created thorough your gifts and talent. More on how to generate money is explained in this entire book.

9. Offer your business as a franchise. To expand and increase sales.

10. Budgeting—Managing and controlling your Finances

The importance of a budget to create wealth.

Tracking your spending

The definition of budgeting-A systematic plan used to track your spending for a given period of time. Budgeting can be associated with why some people have less money to take care of their needs. Budgeting helps to create wealth; therefore, we must help individuals that do not budget their money and understand the power behind budgeting.

People that create a budget have more money than if they didn't implement one. Once an individual accumulates finances, there is a big need associated with managing and controlling it.

This control is called budgeting, and it doesn't matter how much money you have.

How to control your money once you get some? People have won many lotteries and within six months to a year they are broke. No matter whether a person inherited the money or was a successfully businessman, they must know how to manage the cash flow of their money.

First, you must analyze your spending habits. It takes longer to make money than it takes to spend it. You want to watch your credit card spending; especially, due to the high interest rate. Unless you pay your credit card balance off each month, the interest payment becomes more than what you have borrowed. For example, if you borrow $1000 with an interest rate of 12% for 12 months, the bank will make $10 in interest every month until the bill is paid. If the interest rate was 21%, you would pay $17.51 per month in interest. This is the impact the credit cards have in controlling your money. Therefore, you need a budget.

Secondly, you want to have a budget to gain control over your cash inflows and outflows.

By having a budget, it tracks your spending and shows you where you are spending too much money so you can take measures to control that area, (Income vs. Expense).

Thirdly, you will be able to determine your financial position, set specific goals, and be able to achieve them.

Other financial steps to take in managing and controlling your money.

- Set up a separate saving account from your regular checking account.

- Implement direct deposit for your checks to go directly to the bank so your money can be available immediately.

- Open an interest-bearing checking account.

- Open and IRA, Keogh, SEP, or 401-K plan

- Invest in stocks and bonds of various companies

- Invest in certificates of Deposits (CDs)

- Invest in additional real estate properties besides your home

- If your are a Christian, you should always pay 10% of your money earned to God in tithes and offerings, and 10% to self.

- You must prepare a "Will." Estate Planning is very important in managing your income to ensure that your money is properly for the deceased intended. Some people leave donations for nonprofit organizations since contributions are tax deductible.

- Discuss your situation with an accountant, lawyer, Christian financial counselor, financial planner or tax advisor.

On the next few pages, you will see two sample budget forms to use for controlling your money annually and monthly. The following pages (101-102) show a profile of a self-employed person vs. working on a job. Then compare your life and see, which profile fits your present financial status.

The Typical American Family Budget—Monthly

	Husband	Wife	Total
INCOME:			
Salary after Taxes	————	————	————
Business Venture	————	————	————
Savings	————	————	————
Investments	————	————	————
Stock	————	————	————
Mutual Fund	————	————	————
Real Estate	————	————	————
————	————	————	————
————	————	————	————
————	————	————	————
————	————	————	————

FIXED EXPENSES:

Church–Tithes/
      Offerings   _____   _____   _____

Pay-Self   _____   _____   _____

Food   _____   _____   _____

Housing/Rent   _____   _____   _____

Loan Payment   _____   _____   _____

Insurance Premiums
      Health   _____   _____   _____

      Life   _____   _____   _____

Automobiles   _____   _____   _____

Automobile Repairs   _____   _____   _____

Income Tax Payments   _____   _____   _____

Utilities (Gas, Light, Water) _____   _____   _____

Telephone   _____   _____   _____

Credit Card Expenses   _____   _____   _____

Emergency Spending   _____   _____   _____

_____   _____   _____   _____

_____   _____   _____   _____

VARIBLE EXPENSES:
Clothing   ———————   ———————   ———————

Personal Care   ———————   ———————   ———————

Health Care   ———————   ———————   ———————

Entertainment   ———————   ———————   ———————

Vacation   ———————   ———————   ———————

Holidays Spending   ———————   ———————   ———————

Gasoline   ———————   ———————   ———————

Miscellaneous (Will, etc)   ———————   ———————   ———————

———————————————   ———————   ———————   ———————

———————————————   ———————   ———————   ———————

The Typical American Family Budget—Annually

	Husband	Wife	Total
INCOME:			
Salary after Taxes	——	——	——
Business Venture	——	——	——
Savings	——	——	——
Investments	——	——	——
Stock	——	——	——
Mutual Fund	——	——	——
Real Estate	——	——	——
———	——	——	——
———	——	——	——
———	——	——	——
———	——	——	——

FIXED EXPENSES:

Church–Tithes/
    Offerings   _____   _____   _____

Pay-Self   _____   _____   _____

Food   _____   _____   _____

Housing/Rent   _____   _____   _____

Loan Payment   _____   _____   _____

Insurance Premiums
    Health   _____   _____   _____

    Life   _____   _____   _____

Automobiles   _____   _____   _____

Automobile Repairs   _____   _____   _____

Income Tax Payments _____   _____   _____

Utilities (Gas, Light, Water) _____   _____   _____

Telephone   _____   _____   _____

Credit Card Expenses _____   _____   _____

Emergency Spending   _____   _____   _____

_____   _____   _____   _____

_____   _____   _____   _____

VARIBLE EXPENSES:
Clothing   _____   _____   _____

Personal Care   _____   _____   _____

Health Care   _____   _____   _____

Entertainment   _____   _____   _____

Vacation   _____   _____   _____

Holidays Spending   _____   _____   _____

Gasoline   _____   _____   _____

Miscellaneous (Will, etc)   _____   _____   _____

_____   _____   _____   _____

_____   _____   _____   _____

TYPICAL PROFILE OF A SELF-EMPLOYED PERSON CASH FLOW PATTERN VS. WORKING ON A JOB

Income—Consist of
> Dividends
> Interest
> Rental Income
> Royalties
> Residual Income
> Compensation
> Investments
> Real Estates

Expense—Spending
> Food
> Clothes
> Fun
> Property taxes
> Fixed expenses

Asset—Accumulated by Investments		Liability
Stocks Ownership		None
Bonds	Entrepreneurship	Houses are paid
Notes	Tax Deductions	for in bonuses or
		gifts.
Real Estate		Paid Vacations
Network Marketing		
Mutual Funds		

Do you see the benefits and advantages of being self-employed? Yes_____ No_____

Does this profile fit you?_____

If not, why No?_____

TYPICAL PROFILE OF A PERSON WORKING ON A JOB VS. SELF-EMPLOYMENT

Income—Consist of
    Paycheck
    Salary
    2-Jobs (full-time and part-time)

Expense—Spending
    Pay Taxes, Entertainment
    Food, Gasoline
    Rent, Personal Care
    Clothes, Vacation
    Fun
    Baby Sitter
    Fixed Expenses
    Insurance
    Telephone/Cellular/home
    Credit Cards
    Loans
    Automobile
    Utilities

Assets—Investments
    None

Most poor, working, and middle-class
people do not Invest their money, so
they have bills and are in debt to
the creditors.

Liability
Mortgage (house)
Loans
Credit Cards
Car

Do you see the reasons why a person is in debt by working on a job vs. being self-employed? Yes ____ No ____

Does this profile fit you? _____

If not, Why? _____

Major Differences Between

Self-Employed and a Job

Listed are some of the major differences between the self-employed and a person working on a job are:

Self-Employed:
1. The self-employed person has more income and does not work for money.
2. The self-employed person accumulates asset rather than liability.
3. Have a surplus of money to live on and spend.
4. Control own time.
5. Understands how to make money.
6. Live a daily life of wealth and prosperity.
7. Have vision, discipline and is self-motivated.

Person with a Job
1. A person, working on a job, accumulates liability and thinks that they are assets.
2. The person working on a job only income maybe two jobs.
3. Doesn't make enough money to cover all of his bills.
4. Does not control his time; no vision for financial life.
5. Does not understand how to make money or accumulates wealth.

6. Will never achieve wealth with only a job.

7. Usually, not motivated and lack discipline

What differences do you see? List them.

1. _____

2. _____

3. _____

Do you see why you are in debt and will never overcome debt working on a job?

Yes _____ No. _____

Explain your answer: _____

_____

Managing Your Money

Most people don't know how to manage money nor know how to accumulate, or create it.

These questions are designed to help in managing your money.

1. What is the difference between asset and liability?
   • Asset is something that puts money into your pocket
   • Liability is something that takes money from your pocket.

2. What are the differences between a rich and poor person?

- Rich person buys or acquires assets
- Poor person acquires or creates liability and he thinks that he is buying assets.

3. Having more money will solve your problem?
   - It is how you spend and manage your money.

4. Academic success or going to college solves your money problem.
   - More people learn academic skills, but not how to create wealth.

5. The highest income tax paid.
   - Social Security.

6. When you work on a job, wealth is not created and you work from paycheck to paycheck.
   - You must invest in ways for your money to work for money.

7. Some ways for you to create money or wealth.
   - Invest in opportunities and implement your financial vision.

8. Wealth is measured by what?
   - The cash flow from the asset column compared with the expense column

9. To make a decision for your finances, you must understand the world system controlling you.
   - Then you must implement a financial system for your life.

Separate yourself–be different take control of your life.

Beat the rattrap; don't do what other people are doing.

Don't' work for someone else's vision. Everyone has a vision take time to develop it.

Financial lack and struggle are often caused by working for someone else all your life.

Financial Freedom at Last

If your don't give, you don't receive, and "nothing from nothing produces nothing," these statements are true, and I believe we have all heard them. The Bible makes statements like these "Give and it shall be given unto you … and "you reap what you sow." If you don't plant any seeds, don't expect a crop. There is nothing free in this world, and if something is free, it is an increase or a benefit to the person giving the free services or products away.

The world's financial system is setup to dominate and control through economic power. The major economic powers are based on a structure system of communism, socialism, and capitalism. However, whatever system is being used, it has its weaknesses and strengths. In America, we have an economic system based on a capitalist society, which is designed to offer everyone the opportunity to be free and equal. The American system also has an economic career plan for our life (a job), the "American Labor Force" if you don't have a financial future for your life. The America's economic system has a built in plan for supporting the state and Federal Government programs, through a system known as "taxes." In addition, if a person dies without a "Will", the state has an "Estate Plan" for your life. I am making these statements to support the point that in America the "economic system" is so structured and planned through "Uncle Sam" the Federal Government, until what you fail to take control of in your life, the government will control it for you. Everyone needs to understand its economy in order to be able to function and be responsible and accountable for creating a vision for one's own life, and should know how to operate within the guidelines of the government system in taking control of their financial life. Therefore, we must know what economic system we are regulated by, which is "capitalism" in America. Then we must know how it operates and how to utilize the system for our financial advantage to have an abundant life. The concept of a capitalistic society is having ownership and the freedom to be creative. Our system is based on two key things: manufacturing and marketing of goods and services. Then investing your money to create wealth. Under capitalism, working on a job does not allow individuals the opportunity to benefit financially or to charge a set price for working because they receive a salary. Comparing early American history, we see how our economic system has developed and the trends that have taken place that have changed our economy. During the Colonial days, people worked for themselves. Then the labor force emerged with the agricultural, industrial, and manufacturer trends. Shareowners needed people to work for them to plant crops, operate machines, and run factories in order to produce goods and services. In return for labor, people were offered pay for the work they performed. During the industrial period, the economy grew and got so big until people found it easier to go to work in the factory than to start businesses on their own. With growth taking place, a demand and need for laborers increased until people migrated to America to find work. Since people were offered money for labor, many preferred to work versus starting a business of their own. There were many drawbacks for people owning a business. Obtaining cash flow was one and wearing several hats such as being your own accountant and marketing consultant was another, which was very depressing. As time passed, people got farther and farther away from operating their own businesses because it was better and easier to work on a job and get a paycheck rather than running a business, and this was the beginning of the American labor force. Now, the trend, under the technology movement is taking a turn back to the small and home-based businesses. Today, roughly 20 percent of people are in business for themselves. This is due partially to technology and since people are tired of being a part of the labor force. They work hard and see little pay in return for their time. Now people realize that working on a job is not the best solution to get out of debt and obtain wealth since a job creates a slavery mentality and put people in bondage. Therefore, people are looking for avenues that will put them in control of their own lives through entrepreneurship or investments to have asset versus liability. The "Network Generation," accomplished with technology has created a network of people who are creative, intelligent, and who do not have the mindset to work on a job. They are hunger for a better live and are changing the present "status quo " of jobbers. The opportunity is here through technology, and the network generation is taking every advantage of it, and now you can also apply this information in this book to your life and get involve with investment or start your own business or investment. During the earlier days in America, people worked to survive. Now people are working to have extra income for pleasure and to obtain some of the world's luxury resources such as a larger home, a status quo car, and be free of debt. Most people realize that to obtain this type of life style, it is going to take more income than working a job. As we read earlier in previous chapter, this change will effect 80 percent of the American people who work for money to make a living.

The people in the 80 percent category include the working middle-class and college graduates are the people who are taking care of the welfare recipients, the homeless, disadvantaged victims, Medicare and Medicaid patients, immigrants, drug, and alcohol victims, etc. by paying taxes sequentially to working on a job. These people labor faithfully year after year expecting to obtain financial independence when in fact it is inieviable under the circumstances of working on a job. This same insanity is self-perpetuating years after years and 80 percent of American people have fallen into this job trap. This is due to the population growth, lack of understanding the economy system, depending on the government, and failing to take the initiative to implement a career plan of action for your own life. For many years, The American labor force has produced poverty, uselessness, crime, despair, and laziness on the part of most individuals. The American labor force has trapped many people into the jobs, which has created a situation known as, "The Lazy Man Syndrome." This syndrome is a term given to the American people who have depended on the government to ensure that the common masses of people can have work provided for them to do in order to take care of their families. Considering the workers, with thoughts given to the American dream; the job system is more detrimental to the human race, because the human beings were born to be creative beings, not to work for another person on a job. The job has caused individuals to compromise their God-given purpose for life to work for someone else's vision. It also has produced bondage and a slave mentality on the part of most individuals since the majority of the people are so dependent on a job until they cannot function outside of having a job or the next best thing to do is get on welfare. Under our present Government system unless more emphasizes are put on building individual businesses and supporting their efforts to maintain them, capitalism will suffer and the people too. As long as our system continues to promote jobs unto retirement, living from paycheck to paycheck, impoverished conditions will increase. In this society, we find most minorities, men, children, and women who have been rejected from being selected for the better white collar jobs, who have succumb to other measures such as committing crime, selling drugs, being on welfare, and prostitution to make a living. Statistics shows that 97 percent of the minority people make up the labor force vs. only 3 percent of the white race. This has been one of the fallacies of the system and which the government is dealing with in communities today, and the taxes of the workers are going to support the fallacies of our own economic system. We do not need to concentrate on having more people to work on jobs, but our government needs to be concerned about reducing or reversing the number of people having jobs and implement a plan to get more people involved in operating a business to become self-sufficient.

Even the Internal Revenue System defines a taxpayer as one who works for another and is under the control of that individual and these are the people who file W-2's. If you doubt what I am saying, call IRS and ask them to define the people who file W-2's. Working for someone else has created a system in which, it takes very little effort to exert for an individual to get paid. This system of working on a job has been in effect for so long, most people don't consider other alternatives of earning a living. This is why very few people have challenged the system because they are not taught or aware of this information. Our grade schools and colleges do not teach how to benefit and create wealth in a capitalist society to be debt free. We are taught the meaning of capitalism but not how to benefit financially from it. Life is, not suppose to be about—controlling another person's life. Now you can see why so many people are on welfare, drugs, committing crime, and can't find work. A job has and still continues to depress so many people from using their God-given gifts and talents to bless mankind. The American labor force has been and still is one of the leading and strongest networks to discriminate among the races. God has never supported a type of system that caters to slavery, control, bondage, and discrimination. God came to release man from bondage through His Son, Jesus Christ, by way of the Cross. This type of system violates every principle of a free enterprise society. It creates a situation where a person's creative ability is shut-off and mind is reconditioned to another set of plans, which are routine, repetitious, and hinder a person ability to have a better life. The consequences of the American job system have damaged a person's motivation, determination, and desire to achieve his God's given purpose for life. This has affected and created a lazy and dysfunctional mind. This is why I call the job situation the "Lazy Man Syndrome". This syndrome has affected 80 percent of the American people's thinking and has limited and paralyzed their minds from producing visions. The lazy man syndrome is another name

for "slavery" which has stricken a person creative ability by a rees-
tablished plan from birth to retirement, and to death. The majority of the people don't escape the "Lazy Man Syndrome" trap until
they die since most people even after retirement still need money
to survive and have no choice but to work. This is because the
majority of the workers do not invest any money while they were
working and they retire broke. Statistics show that 97 percent of
the people retire broke and still need a job to obtain money until
they die. Due to the Technology Age, people might be able to
retrain their mind and seek work by starting businesses instead of
looking for a job. At least by writing this book, it exposes the
consequences and repercussions of a job in achieving wealth. It is
up to the individual to decide his career and economic status and
make a choice for their life.

Success doesn't discriminate it is always leading you on a jour-
ney. People have different abilities, goals, and desires, and what
motivate or drive them is one of the deciding factors in a person's
life to escape the American job trap and pursue his dream. It is
easy to get complacency about what we do, to get locked into solving
needs, and to get busy with activities that keeps a person in bondage.

I recommend that everyone seeking to a better life read this
book "Rich Dad Poor Dad" by Robert T. Kiyosaki with Sharon L.
Lechter C.P.A. There are many things in this book to give you
insight and ways to get out of debt and become financial secure. I
found that after reading this book, there were many things the
authors and I shared, but this passage that supports my previous
statements is as follow:

> "The No. 1 expense for most people is taxes. Many
> people thank it is income tax, but for most Americans their
> highest tax is Social Security. As an employee, it appears as
> if the Social Security tax combine with the Medicare tax
> rate is roughly 7. 5 percent, but it is really 15 percent since
> the employer must match the Social Security amount. In
> essence, it is money the employer cannot pay you. On top

of that, you still have to pay income tax on the amount deducted from your wages for Social Security tax, income you never receive because it went directly to Social Security through withholding."

In Summary:

When you work for someone else, you are working for that person's dream, success, and retirement; and no matter whom you work for, it will always be to benefit that person's life. The more and harder you work, the more taxes are taken from your paycheck to support more government programs. You don't make more money by working more hours or by working two jobs because it does not do anything, except increases your tax bracket for paying more taxes. Therefore, you are back where you started because working on two or more jobs don't increase your assets it increases your taxes and debts. When individuals work on a job, 'they are taxed on what they earn, what they spend, what they save, and when they die," in *Rick Dad Poor Dad* by Robert T. Kiyosaki and co-authored by Sharon L. Lechter. Learn to work smarter by owning your own business and investing into their future.

Keep this in mind when making a decision to make life better for yourself, you should know that almost all of the financial struggles are directly associated with working on a job all of your life for someone else. If you want to make changes in your financial future, you must consider a job versus starting a business to live an abundant life on earth.

Sixteen Reasons Why People Are in Their Current Financial Situation

1. Programmed to work on a job vs. self-employment
2. Not a part of a support network that will allow opportunity, flexibility, and financial growth
3. Don't want to take the initiative to change
4. Fear of change or failure

5. No vision or plan to succeed in life
6. Don't understand a capitalist society
7. Passive not active–Dependency on other people for their financial well being in life
8. Not expanding knowledge and skills
9. See only one way of making a living and that is working on a job for money
10. Insufficient knowledge for achieving personal wealth accumulation
11. Taught to be dependent vs. independent under the America's job system
12. Not able to manage their money
13. Negative Attitude
14. Not focus
15. Living on a limited income
16. Being locked into a define economic labor force–working for someone else who reaps the financial benefits

What Is Economic Empowerment?

Being Open To Opportunities

Controlling Your Financial Future

Financially Secure

Improved Financial Life

Sufficiency of Disposal Income

Some Problems Associated With People Lacking Money

1. Divorce
2. Stress
3. Stealing
4. Sickness
5. Isolation of Self
6. Isolation of Others
7. Lies
8. Lack of Happiness
9. Negative Attitude
10. Poor Self-Image of Self
11. Homelessness
12. Often Depressed
13. Live in Disparity
14. High Debts
15. Insufficient income to meet families needs
16. Commit Crimes
17. Depend upon drugs and alcohol
18. Become a dependent of the Government Assistance Programs

Some Barriers Associated With Operating a Business

1. Insufficient Cash Flow
2. Limited access to financial resource to start a business
3. Limited knowledge on how to manage the daily operation of the business
4. Not Truthful and Honest in dealing with Customers
5. Not providing quality services
6. Not networking with other businesses
7. A history of bad credit and debts
8. Not hiring a good staff
9. Trying to do everything yourself

How to Overcome Barriers?

1. Do a Business plan
2. Find other people who will invest into your vision
3. Create or invent a products that you think will sell
4. Check with relatives and friends to invest into your business
5. Get other knowledgable people to work for you
6. Network with others
7. Always pray

Some types of businesses you can start with few barriers are listed in my book, *Federal Income Taxes and the Small BusinessPerson,* see how to order a copy at the end of this book.

Twenty-One Reasons Why Most Businesses Fail

1. Limited budget to start a business
2. Insufficient Cast flow
3. Lack of marketing plan to increase customers
4. Lack of networking with other businesses
5. Not trusting in God
6. Lost of desire or vision to continue business
7. Lack of Business Plan
8. Not expanding knowledge and skills
9. Not coachable
10. Lack of follow-up system in place to track customers
11. Not able to build and keep a qualified staff
12. Failure to keep up with the economic changes in technology
13. No demand for products and services
14. Poor management and no structure program
15. Fast turnover rate of trained employees
16. Lack of expansion plan for growth
17. One person business operation

D

18. Trying to wear four hats (Manager, accountant, lawyer, and marketer)
19. No focus
20. Lack of discipline and poor attitude
21. Give up

How to Keep Your Business from Falling?

1. Come up with a super idea
2. Have a marketable product or service
3. Put the business plan into effect
4. Do a business for a sole proprietorship or corporation
5. Recruit partners in other areas of expertise
6. Invest some of your saving you have in the bank for seed money
7. Establish a budget
8. Build an excellent customer service branch, and you will always have customers who are loyal
9. Always pray for your business to glorify God to be a success
10. Don't try to do everything by yourself; get the necessary people to work with you such as an accountant, secretary, lawyer, marketing representative and other people to be on your team
11. Take time for training and send your staff to training.
12. Do your work for fun; don't over work yourself; and spend quality tine with family
13. Find people that share the same vision that you can trust.
14. Be caring and work friendly with staff in meeting their personal needs

Five Key Steps to Help a Person Succeed in Business

Paul J, Myers's five "Million Dollar Personal Success Plan"

I. Crystallize Your Thinking

    Determine what specific goal you want to achieve. Then dedicate yourself to its attainment with unswerving singleness of purpose, the trenchant zeal of a crusader.

II. Develop a Plan for Achieving Your Goal, and a Deadline for its Attainment

    Plan your progress carefully; hour-by-hour, day-by-day, month-by-month. Organized activity and maintained enthusiasm are the wellsprings of your power.

III. Develop a Sincere Desire for the Things You Want in Life

    A burning desire is the greatest motivator of every human action. The desire for success implants " success consciousness" which, in turn, creates a vigorous and ever-increasing habit of success."

IV. Develop Supreme Confidence in Yourself and Your Own Abilities.

    Enter every activity without giving mental recognition to the possibility of defeat.
    Concentrate on your strengths, instead of your weaknesses . . . on your powers, instead of your problems.

.D

V. Develop a Dogged Determination to Follow Through on Your Plan, Regardless of Obstacles, Criticism or Circumstances or What Other People Say, Think or Do

> Construct your Determination with Sustained Effort, Controlled Attention, and Concentrated Energy.
> **Opportunities never come to those who wait . . . they are captured by those who dare to ATTACK.**

CHAPTER 4–WHY CHRISTIANS SHOULD GET INVOLVED IN NETWORK MARKETING?

This section is especially for all Christian Readers

Delivered Out of Egypt

God delivered His people out of bondage when he led them out of Egypt once and for all, but the majority of people are back in Egypt by the craftiness of the American economic system. Especially, the Christians because they are being controlled through time and money by a spirit of control to keep them in bondage. The world economic system is set up for dominion, leadership control, and economic dependency by keeping people enslaved to working on a job. It is easy, however, for a person to get caught up in the American economic system because it is structured to provide jobs for people and at the same time control their destiny, and this is the devil's purpose to keep Christians in bondage. However, far too many pastors and Christians do not perceive working on a job as bondage, because they have not been made aware of some of the things mentioned in this book. The Bible states that if you don't work to take care of your own you are worse than an infidel in I Timothy 5:8, but missing from this statement is that pastors and Christians have tied this scripture to working on a job. However, there are other sources of work that are not associated with a job. Some Christians view a job as the only best and legal way to make a living and they are satisfied with their present conditions. This is good, but we must desire to come into the full knowledge of God's perfect will for the Christian's life. It is easy to fall into the American labor trap since it takes no investment to find a job; but it does take money to pursue your dreams. This is why the majority of people look for a job to perform rather than start a business. In addition, they are disciplined and brainwashed toward working for money and someone else and are not self-motivated to fulfill their dreams. In fact, a job has become a way of life for 80 percent of the American people. However, this should not be the case for Christians since they should be minding their own business in accordance to the scriptures, which reads "And that ye study to be quiet, and to do your own business and to work with your own hands, as we commanded you." (I Thessalonians 4: 1). I thank God for inventing jobs since it has been a blessing for me, but also it has hindered me from achieving my dream in life as Christ has intended for me to live. Now, I am pursuing my dream and like every bit of controlling my own time and not having to live by a clock. I just what to share with you how to live your life in and with Christ. If you are presently working on a job or looking for one now, reread this book until your mind is renew and you are taking control of your life. If you need help, call Families United for Restoration, Inc., the staff will be glad to help you achieve your dream in life. If you are thinking about changing your financial future from a job to a business, get some help. There are all types of help for you and you don't have to work on a job all your life since a job is not designed for permanent income to live an abundant life. Consider the position or the reasons of a job below and count the cost for your life:

> A job should not be a mean to an end
> A job should be a mean to a beginning to self-employment

A job should be temporary for obtaining seed money to
   improve your future

A job should be used only until you can do better and never
   to retirement

A job should mean supplemental income to meet a special
   need

A job should be a mean to obtain a skill to start your own
   business

A job should be a way to get experience and connection to
   achieving your personal goals

Self-Employment

I was inspired to write this chapter in this book by the unction of the Holy Spirit to share with Christians how to become financially secure and bring greater insight to why many Christians are not living a successful life as they have dreamed or anticipated. It is not God's desire for Christians to be working on a job because it creates bondage and not financial freedom. The more you work the more spending it takes, the more taxes you pay, and the more liability you assume. We must create wealth according to God's principles in Genesis 1: 11-12 by planting a seed to start a business. God 's system is for Christians to create a vision for obtaining wealth on earth for their lives. To obtain more knowledge, understanding for finding your purpose in life, I recommend you to purchase my book "Breaking the Financial Curse of Poverty Over Your Life, Entrepreneurship: A Divine Calling from God and the American Dream, " co-authored with Dr. Betty Lancaster-Short.

This book will focus you in the right path of understanding God's purpose for living and to reaping an abundant life. Many Christians have missed the mark big time, so have I? However, I was privileged to read an article entitled " Who Decides Students' Future?" School-to-Work Law Gets Heavily Involved, in the "Investor's Business Daily," Thursday August 27, 1998, issue, which states that the School-To-Work program was going to be revamped. Children will be trained to the workplace early in their life starting with kindergarten relevant to real-life, real-work situations. The present School-to-Work program is structured around occupations, occupational types, and workers–worker bees– not entrepreneurs and competitors. The program will receive $150 million from the Government for 1999. "Samuel L. Blumenfeld, an education writer and expert stated, "He feels there should be more of entrepreneurs training rather than around the worker bees. He further states that many people are saying, "Isn't this nice– they are helping their children get jobs."–When in fact they don't realize it violates every principle of a free society." He feels that children are taught basic training skills and sent out in the world to make a living for themselves. Then the government will plan their life for them and the children will not become highly liberated nor financially independent individuals.

I was very much impressed by Mr. Blumenfeld's remarks and I am including the article in this section to support my position's concerning self-employment should be taught vs. job from an early age. God said train up a child and he shall not depart from it. So, I believe Christians should be bringing up their children in the way of the Lord. Therefore, I agree with Mr. Blumenfeld that unless this type of training is changed, the majority of our children will always be depending on the government to take care of them, as some people are today. I believe this is why people are the way they are in life. This confirms my statements of how this type of system can polarized the mind of our children early by creating dependency upon the government, producing a syndrome of laziness and despair rather than supporting a system that promotes independent living through God-given gifts and talents for every human being. When people can't find a job, they depend upon the warfare, which makes people lazy if they are not using their creative abilities to its fullest capacity. Secondly, they become less motivated and disciplined toward taking control of their financial future. And thirdly, they disconnect themselves from society and become a burden by using other types of action to counteract the system; such as committing robberies, murders and suicide. This is the result produced when people are taught to work for money instead of teaching them early in life ways of how to obtain money other than working on a job. A job is not for everyone even though an individual needs money. Some people do better by working for themselves fixing hair or cutting hair or by working on a farm. These are occupations that we should encourage.

Children need to be taught the meaning of money early in life and how to use their talents and gifts in starting their own businesses and not be supported by the government. The parents could be a great example in this area, but most parents do not own a business. Therefore, many children are not exposed to this type of environment nor get first hand experience to imitate or duplicate their parents' businesses. Living in the technology and/or information age, we see more people are moving back into the home-based and small businesses at the adult level. Nevertheless, but we need to expose this type of training to our children at an early stage of a child's life. However, the Federal government must take the lead by incorporating entrepreneurship classes in our schools. When a child reaches Junior High School, he should be tested as to the type of self-employment occupational gift. Then school counselors should match the students with a company that can train and help them pursue their dream. This procedure should be done for people with more emphasis on starting a business for self-employment. As every thing else it takes a type of discipline to run a business. Therefore, there should be a system to help screened the students to identify their talent and potential. If these students have dropped out of school, they should attend a trade school to take up a skill for a service job and be hired as an independent contractor, not an employee. Upon completing their training, then support these individuals financially and help them become partner with a company to help him achieve their dream or support from their local government. It has been in the past, that when students don't have the academic ability to become a doctor or lawyer, this individual is thrown in a business class or they drop out of school and becomes a store clerk or janitor.

There should be a training program in place for these drop-outs to support these young entrepreneur students to help them get started in a business that will offer them a more challenging position in life. The government should work with network mark-ing companies, nonprofits, and churches as other sources of help-ing individuals to create business opportunities as independent distributors or contractors. We find many gifted young people searching for financial support to help them to launch an idea or vision with very little support. The venture capitals are mainly for servicing the ivory league people and not for the minorities. It has been and still is tough for women to get the financial support needed to start a business. Even though we know that there are millions of dollars to support people who are trying to start a busi-ness by venture capitals, Small Business Association, Angels, etc., but to actual get the money is like trying to find a needle in a hay stacked. This should not be the case. All of these so-called govern-mental programs only support the people who are involved in get-ting the grants and loans, which should not be the case. Today, there still a need or a cry for individuals who are more at risk to get the financial backing to start their business if you are in the low-to-middle class minority families. I never understood why the gov-ernment would rather give away money to people on welfare as oppose to those starting a business lacking collateral or seed money.

In a capitalist society, it is actually the inventors and entrepre-neurs, large and small businesses, and home-based business own-ers who are running the country, not the workers and the welfare recipients. Therefore, money should be appropriated in the gov-ernment budget to help more people start businesses and set up support systems to help and encourage them to be successful in their business. This is another breakdown of the American system to not have funds set aside to help people who want to create wealth. There are many benefits to owning a business, such as a tax deduction, less welfare, and a better distribution of wealth. It is good to have a welfare system to help the poor because God speaks of this in the Bible, but we must train and support the welfare recipients to produce income instead of consuming income. We must afford them equal opportunity to start businesses as for working on a job.

If America continues to give to the poor and not support entrepreneur ventures and self-employment, this nation can become broke without supporting efforts of the working class people. The working class people pay taxes, take care of the poor, and keep the government running, but many are never able to achieve an abundant life for themselves because of our system.

Network Marketing Opportunities for Welfare recipients:

Everything is a network system including working on a job. Christians and other people should get more involve in promoting network marketing opportunities as a source to create wealth for church members, welfare recipients, and families who may or may not qualify for working on a job.

Network Marketing Opportunities for Christians:

I perceive in my spirit that network marketing is a special gift from God to create the atmosphere where people can get off of welfare and God's people can carry out His mandate and program on earth. Christians can not work for God and Uncle Sam (serve two masters) at the same time and be effective in winning souls and have time with God and rest. "No man can serve two masters; for either he will hate the one, and love the other; or else he will hold to one, and despise the other. Ye cannot serve God and money. " (Matthew 6:24) It is hard to operate a business and work on a job. Some point in time you must give up the job and run (mind) your own business because this is where the Christians will be blessed. Most of the Christian men and women are busy, rushing, and only have time to be ministered to, and not ministered to others. The average or typical schedule for Christians is to be at church on Sunday mornings and evenings; work through the week-days from Monday through Friday doing the day. Attend women meeting on Monday nights; take child to Soccer practice on Tues-day nights; Bible study on Wednesday nights; prayer meeting on Thursday nights; church meeting and/or youth meetings on Fri-day nights; church's prayer breakfast and soccer games Saturday mornings and Saturday evenings, choir practice. Reviewing this sample schedule, no wonder the devil wants you working on a job. When is there time to minister to the lost with a schedule similar to this one? Most people only have time to do two things: go to work and to church if they are Christians with a few sport activi-ties on the weekends. This is the typical American life style that the devil has planned for us. "And the cares of this world and the deceitfulness of riches, and the lusts of other things entering in, choke the word and it become unfruitful." (Mark 4:19). If the devil can keep stealing your time and keep the Christians believ-ing that a job is your only source of income, then he has won the biggest battle over your life. If we can get more people to get in-volve with God's plan of work of self-employment, then the Chris-tians will win, and some would reap thirty-fold and some sixty and some a hundred return of everything they touch. Most people's schedule keep them so busy until they hardly have enough time for their families, time to pray, and minister for God. Very few people deviate from the sample schedule, and this is how they live until they die. And this is not the life God wants us to live; at least, not for me. I have a greater vision than this for my life, and this is why I have positioned myself to take control of my time, and money.

To move a person from a job mentality to owning a business will take time, prayer, and a lot of faith. The person must see God's "vision" for establishing wealth. A vision is caught and not taught. The church must stop endorsing getting a job and getting Christians in bondage to the world system. It must endorse a program that will generate wealth for God's people, by promoting a system where money can work for people as Elisha, told the widow woman. Well, if you say, Sister Ann that will not work for today's economy. Then I know your church missed the vision. But if you say yes, we must do it God's way, then your church has received the vision. The Bible is the same today, yesterday and tomorrow, it will never change. We know that you cannot move a person from their job, but this book is to bring truth to those people seeking financial independence and haven't received it yet. The scripture says " Thus saith the Lord of hosts: Consider your ways." (Haggai 1:7) Therefore, it is time to consider your ways and be willing to pay the cost. If statistics show that 80 percent of the population is in bondage to a job, then you have to initiate change do what 20 percent of the people are doing who are living their dreams and are not in bondage. The different between the two groups of people is that the 80 percent group is working for money and the 20 per-cent group has money working for them because they are self-employed. The key different is being self-employed.

The easiest way to become self-employed is through a net-work marketing companies as explained in this book and there are no qualifications that will eliminate no one. Not only is network legal, but it is a business that allows your money to work for you, an investment, and is endorsed by God. Christian friends, it is good to have great respect for your pastors, but some of them are not hearing God's word concerning how to increase your finances to be prosperous in the eyes of God. This is keeping you in bond-age spiritually and financially unless you are hearing from God for yourself. This is why God made it plain that each person is re-sponsible for working out its own salvation with God. God is not just speaking of financial matters but spiritual matters at well. Having prosperity is strictly part of God's salvation plan. Creflo Dollar said, "you are not completely whole until you have over-come the world in your finances. There is no peace living from paycheck to paycheck and worrying about paying your rent and high credit card debts."

If you are presently working on a job and are looking for a way to help you to get out of debt and get in God's plan, try a network marketing companies. I know network marketing opportunities have been viewed negative by most Christians, and many who have tried network marketing have not been successful because they didn't understand that it is a plan of God to help people to get out of debt and it was hard to recruit other people. Based upon negative remarks, not seeing the vision, and having the money to invest, have reflected very negative toward people pursuing a network business. This is exactly what the devil wants to do and that is to discredit network marketing opportunities, so you can continue to work for him and he can control your time, money, and life style. The devil tries to discredit everything that God does good for his people to overcome the world. The devil tries to get people from being saved and filled with the Holy Spirit. And may I say, because you are in a church, it doesn't mean that you are saved and filled, unless your have confessed Jesus as your Lord and Savior with your mouth and believed in your heart that He died for you on the cross. Then asked Him to filled you or empowered you with His Holy Spirit. Being in a local church doesn't make any one saved without that confession, see Romans 10: 9-13. We need that confession to allow dependency on Christ for our businesses. If your church has not been teaching this, then it must change its teaching to the truth and come into agreement with God's plan of salvation to set people free financially. It is time to let the members know that network marketing is not a pyramid, and the different between a legal vs. an illegal business. We must get member to teach the truth about the position of a job and how to start a business. The church should research to find a good network marketing opportunity. Then select a person to coordinate the group in the church and teach the members how to accumulate wealth for themselves and the people in their community and get off of welfare into homes they can be proud of. The church should not only preach on tithing and offering, but on God's plan of salvation for finances and how to accumulate wealth. God said,

"My people are destroyed for lack of knowledge"–but he, further said in that same verse that my people have rejected knowledge." (Hosea 4:6) We know people reject knowledge based on other people limitations of the word of God. This is why it is so important to read the word for yourself and pray and ask the Holy Spirit to interpret it for you. Network marketing not only builds financial growth, but strong bonds of unity and relationships among members as in Genesis 11: 1, 4, 6, 7 and 9. This was the power of the pagan peoples, but how much more will God build his people a tower of wealth to establish his covenant on earth. This why the devil is trying to keep the church from uniting because he already knows the strength and power behind numbers and volumes. Start a network marketing business in your church, and repent for disobedience and ask God to give you wisdom and knowledge where to find a good network marketing opportunity or call the telephone number at the end of the book.

Network marketing opportunities create economic empowerment for churches and families. Instead of the churches selling candy and chicken dinners, they can support a network within their church that benefits the church, the pastor, and its members. Many churches have endorsed network-marketing opportunities and are flourishing. The reason churches should promote network marketing is because it is a phase of leadership that people can trust and help each other build wealth through an organization where more than one person can benefit from the effort. It is up to the church to teach the principle of wealth through self-employment to help individuals overcome the spirit of struggling and poverty. The church as an institution and should be promoting ways to create sound businesses by turning jobs into businesses and pushing job placement to a minimum. More about the gift and talent of God should be taught to help people find their purpose in life. The network marketing "vision" is a blessing from God to the church because it is an opportunity to leverage your time and money. When God said in Malachi 3: 10, "...I will open windows in heaven that there shall not be room enough to receive it." He meant he would be opening up opportunities through visions. God has designed a system for all men to create wealth through our own creative being. God has gifted everyone with a special purpose for existing on earth for blessing other people. However, no matter what business we venture into, the devil wants to try to make it hard for Christian families to escape the job trap. The moment a Christian makes a decision to start a business, the devil with his principalities and powers try to stop them from succeeding. Therefore, Christians must beware of some of his tricks, which are: that's a pyramid, you don't have the money to invest, no time to spent in the business, that's not for me, and you are going to lose money on that investment. Any good legal opportunity to be self-employed should not be turned down if you desire to work for yourself. All good opportunities are miracles and blessings from God for His children to succeed and have a successful life and not lack any needs financially in life on earth.

How to Get Out of Egypt?

(Freedom from Working on a Job)

1. Get a "vision" for your financial future from God.
2. Get involved in a business; become an employer vs. an employee.
3. Be willing to plant a seed (Invest some Money).
4. Learn when to use other people's money (OPM).
5. Find others to support your vision or purpose.
6. Network with others; Form Alliance Teams.
7. Start a business that will meet the needs of others.
8. Be a big giver to God and to others in need.
9. Take control of your own destiny in life. Trust in the Lord.
10. Renew your mind and apply information that you have learned in your life.
11. Be willing to admit that you are wrong. Then change your directions.

12. Do your own research. Be accountable and responsible to self.
13. Be willing to exercise your faith or take risk.
14. Read your road map, The Bible. Then apply it to your financial future.
15. Be a prayer warrior. Join a prayer network.
16. Be graceful and give thanks to God. Always depends on God.
17. Know how to identify the enemy of hindrance and bind his work over your life.
18. Work with your own hands and walk in faith and not in fear.

Seventeen Reasons Churches Should Get Involve In Network Marketing Business

1. It offers a system for God to multiply wealth back to you.
2. You have tax deductions available as business owners.
3. It offers an opportunity to become a business owner.
4. It requires no college education.
5. It is a way to get out of debt and stay out.
6. It opens a door to take control of your life.
7. It offers an opportunity for your money to work for you.
8. It is a way to circulate your money instead of accumulating it.
9. It offers an opportunity for people to help each other.
10. It eliminates depression, divorces, and poverty.
11. It opens the door for a quality life and an equal opportunity for everyone.
12. It offers financial independence.
13. It offers a write-off for your business fees.
14. To have time to witness for God.
15. To have money to lend to others in need.
16. To get paid money on overrides, bonuses, commission that are tax deductible.
17. It is part of the technology revolution to make a living in the near future.

Understanding the Key to Prosperity From a Spiritual Aspect

God wants the church to not only be concerned with the spiritual growth of a man, but with his total well being, which is inclusive of all aspects of his life financially, socially, morally, physically, socio-economically, materially, and mentally.

Most people and especially Christians and the middle-class families spend their whole life working for money, but never obtaining wealth. They spend more and build liability. They worry about the lack of insufficient income and how they are going to pay their debt. Some people pay their tithes and offerings and wonder when God is going to do something for them. It is a desire for most women to be home to raise their children in accordance with God's plan and to have the best of material things on earth. They pray, wait, and hope for a breakthrough that never comes, because very few people including Christians act on the word of God with faith. Paying tithes is one aspect of receiving, but we must activate faith into the situation and get involved with some of the windows of opportunities that God has opened in the world such as network marketing, stocks, and mutual funds to get out of debt. In other words, what we need to do is get out of debt and live a debt free life on earth. God said, "According as His divine power has given unto us all things pertaining unto life and Godliness through the knowledge of Him that has called us to glory and virtue." (II Peter 1:3)

People are looking, waiting, and expecting something to come to them, and God has already come and given us a plan to obtain wealth. However, unless we understand how God's plan works, we will continue to pay tithes and offering and still never come into wealth by working on a job. We have to do something besides a job to activate God 's financial plan for us to receive unlimited measures from heaven in faith. We can't limit God or change his plan for our life because of our ignorance of lack of revelation knowledge. One example of how to activate your faith to create wealth is what the Lord, told the widow woman as listed below:

The scripture states, (1) "Now there cried a certain woman of the wives of the sons of the prophets unto Elisha, saying, Thy servant, my husband, is dead, and thou knowest that thy servant did fear the Lord; and the creditor is come to take unto him my two sons to be slaves. (2) And Elisha said unto her, What shall I do for thee? Tell me, *what hast thou in the house?* And she said, Thine handmaid hath not anything in the house, except a pot of oil. (3) Then he said, *Go borrow* thee vessels from all thy neighbors, even empty vessels; borrow not a few. (4) And when thou art come in thou shalt shut the door upon thee and upon thy sons, and shalt pour out into all those vessels, and thou shalt set aside that which is full. (5) So she went from him, and shut the door upon her and upon her sons, who brought the vessels to her; and she poured out. (6) And it came to pass, when the vessels were full, that she said unto her son, bring me yet a vessel. And he said unto her, There is not a vessel more. And the oil stopped flowing, and (7) Then she came and told the man of God. And he said, *Go, sell the oil,* and pay the debt, and live thou and they children on the rest." (II King 4:1-7)

I interpret this scripture as God was talking to me today. I believe this woman had been praying to God and she had been giving her tithes and offering, and was in right standing, but she believes she had not gotten her answer from God. The Lord had heard her prayer the moment she prayed and the answer to the prayer was right in her house, but she needed to know what to do. As with most Christians, the answer to prayer is already there within our reach. Her Husband had been working for money all of his life and assumed nothing but liability and debt; and when he died, they were in so much debt to more than one creditors; probably he owed for his house, car, furniture, several loan officers, and credit cards. His wife probably didn't work on a job and was wondering how she was going to pay the debt. We find a lot of people in this type of situation today. They work for money instead of money

134

working for them, and if something should happen to the Head of Household, they would probably lose everything they have. A lot of people do not have insurance to cover them incase of a death of a husband or wife, so the comparison of this story is that her husband worked for money and accumulated nothing all of his life but liability. But notice this, the Lord didn't tell the widow woman to leave her home and go and get a job to pay the creditors. Because she knew getting a job was not God's perfect will and working for money cause the situation to get worse. The job was the reason why they were in so much debt to the creditors. So, to get out of debt the Lord didn't tell her to go and get a job or get two jobs. Because working on a job all that time hadn't worked in their life, so why would God tell her to find a job now to get them out debt. She can't get out of debt the way they got in debt. The most she could do was create more debt and liability. Doesn't this sound like many of the Christians today? Even if God had told you or me to get the oil, we probably wouldn't have gotten the oil but would have gone looking for a job. We would have disobeyed God and denied that God was speaking to us. We have a chance to make it right now because this is the same message of this book, "get your oil and not a job." Avoid the American job trap because it will cause an increase in liability and debt. Do something to discover your gift or talent and market it. God will be with you the same as with the widow woman.

God had Elisha to tell the widow woman how to pay off her debt other than working on a job. It was through self-employment. God wanted her to use her creative ability to pay off her debt by becoming self–employed through selling the oil because all the increase would go to her in unlimited amounts. God blesses His people through providing a need. For those people who are in business today, I believe God wants you to hang on to your business because unlimited amounts are coming to you. This let everyone knows that self-employment is the way of the spirit, and if you want to continue to work on your job, then it is up to you to go ahead and disobey God and stop complaining about your debt not being paid. The lesson learned and steps Elisha told the widow to follow were to:

- Change the system or source of making money: Don't work for money.

- Get a vision for making money with your hands.

- Do you have any thing tangible that you can do that someone else needs that can be exchanged in return for a monetary value? She had a bottle of oil.

- She knew God voice and was able to hear His voice when God spoke to her.

- She was obedience to God's voice and didn't question it.

- God has someone always present to help and support you.

- She took action mixed with her faith and went and got the oil.

- She was able to follow instructions; Go and borrow the vessel you need and get plenty. Sometimes you may need to borrow the cash you don't have to start your own business.

- She was bold and knew she must make a personal deliver to meet the needs of the community by selling the oil. She sold it or market the oil to the people

- She was a praying women; had a relationship with God; and in constant communion with God.

People must live by God's financial plan so they can have the best of things in life and not by the world system of getting a job. The scripture states "But seek ye first the kingdom of God and all his righteousness and all these things shall be added unto you." (Matthew 6:33) God's kingdom for his people is given through talents, gifts, and abilities for creating work with their hands, so His people can survive on earth without becoming a slave to any man. God's word says," But thou shall remember the Lord thy God, it is who give you power (ability, ideas, and inventions) to get wealth, that He may establish His covenant which He swore unto thy fathers, as it is this day." (Deuteronomy 8:18). Also God will give witty invention through visions and dreams. The words state, "And it shall come to pass afterward, that I will pour out my Spirit upon all flesh, and your sons and your daughters shall prophesy, your old men shall dream dreams, your young men shall see visions." (Joel 2: 28) Ask God's Holy Spirit to anoint your dreams and visions for receiving prosperity to increase your financial harvest, so you can be blessed and you will have enough to bless others because this is the way to turn God's hand toward you to live the life God intended for you. God wants His people blessed and He will reveal things to them for achieving their purpose in life through dreams and visions to be fulfilled on earth. Many people are living their dream today and you can too.

Some dreams can be evil, but we must be able to distinguish between an evil dream or vision and a good dream or vision. A good dream or vision from God is always something positive that is designed to help or to warn people of danger. A spiritual person usually is given visions and dreams from God for discernment, word of knowledge, and word of wisdom to help people spiritually discern things and the period of times in the Bible, see I Corinthians 12:1-11. A dream or vision from God will always line-up or be confirmed by His word, and sometimes they can be so strange until you need a spiritual interpretation of the vision or dream. However, you can rest for sure a dream or vision from God will come to pass. Let us become thinkers and dreamers and change the world.

How to Recognize God-given Visions and Dreams?

Some of this information is taken from one of Benny Hinn's brochures on dream and visions and I thought it would be helping to understand dream and vision and how they related to achieving your finances in life.

A. Dreams:

Dream can come from:

- God: As a result of the outpouring of the Holy Spirit. (Acts 2:17)

- The natural realm: Resulting from a multitude of business. (Ecclesiastes 5:7)

- The demonic realm: From Satan—to defile your flesh. (Jude 1:8) They often concern sexual acts and always result in corruption.

You can always tell when a dream is from God:
It will leave a lasting impression on you. (Genesis 40)
God-given dreams have purpose:
- They reveal God's plans. (Genesis 15:1-22)

- They enable Spirit-directed communication. (Genesis 20:1-7 and 1 Kings 3:5-10) When you are asleep, God speaks through you by the Holy Spirit to give divine directions, which you should act upon in obedience. (Jeremiah 23:28)

- Dreams warn of impending trouble. (Job 33:12-22)

- Dreams establish prophetic revelation. (Job 33:14 and Genesis 41:1-8, 32)

- Acting upon God-given dreams brings prosperity. (Job 36:5-12)

- Dreams provide guidance. (Numbers 12:6)

- Dreams provide battle strategies: (In Judges 7:9-15), Gideon was preparing to fight a tremendous battle against a formidable army. He heard two men talking about a dream, recognized it was from God, acted upon it, and God gave Him victory.

B. Visions

Visions also come as a result of the outpouring of the Holy Spirit. (Acts 2:17)

Four distinguishing characteristics of a God-given vision:

- A vision reveals God's glory. (Isaiah 6:5)

- A vision reveals your own frailty. (Isaiah 6:5)

- A vision will leave you astonished and numb for days. (Ezekiel 1-3)

- A vision will always be followed by an interpretation. (Daniel 7:1,28)

Five Steps For Making a Vision a Reality

- Pray. (Habakkuk 2:1)

- Write the vision and make it plain. (Habakkuk 2:2)

- Act upon it. (Habakkuk 2:2)

- Wait for it. (Habakkuk 2:3)

- Don't lose faith. (Habakkuk 2:3-4)

If you want God to give you dreams and visions and make them clear to you, you must be faithful to Him and His word, as Moses was. (Numbers 12:6-8) Set aside some time and ask the Lord your purpose or gift on earth to mankind. I believe that we all have a God-given gift and that God only reveals it to us through dreams and visions. God wants to speak to His people through the Holy Spirit. God is telling us to use your God-given talents and gifts and come out of bondage by starting you own business. God wants to anoint and increase your business, but if you are not in the position to receive, God cannot increase you. God does not want to put more wealth into the hands of the wicked, nor a Christian that is not connected to His financial system of giving tithes and offering. God has given us all these blessings and it is up to us to pursue them and use them. Therefore, you must plant a seed by starting a business or something that you can do. Learn how to work and build together and depend and support one another. This is the God-given system that God wants to bless. The church's biggest problem is coming together in unity (learning how to network), and then we can possess the land and be blessed to be a blessing. The church has nothing to fear, because God will be with it until the end of time. If you have not been using your God-given talent and gifts to His glory, pray this prayer and ask God to forgive you. He will restore everything back to you and give you a new beginning.

Prayer for Rivers of Financial Blessings

Father, I repent and ask you to forgive me for being ignorant of your word in handling and taking control of my financial life.

Lord I ask your Holy Spirit to deliver me from all dead works, deceitful, bondage, lying, hindrance, stealing, and devourer spirits over my financial life. Lord, I ask your Holy Spirit to anoint me and manifest your purpose for my life. Release your visions, and witty invention of how I should fulfill my purpose on this earth. Remove me now from the bondage of poverty, impoverished conditions and the controlling spirits of working for money on a job and put me in the position to work for myself, as an entrepreneur. Lord, as I plant my seed to start a business in faith, I expect to receive a 100-fold return on my investment in accordance with your word. Lord anoints me with influence to help others to start a business and get out of debt. I thank you that I don't have to work for money, because money works for me as you have planned. Lord, I thank you for giving me favor with men on earth to help me to accomplish my tasks and for supplying all my financial needs and resources to start my business or ministry. Lord I thank you for putting me on the right path for my life so I can build your kingdom on earth. Thank you Lord, I love you and I am putting all my trust in you, not in man. Lord I know that you more than able to make all grace abound toward me. In Jesus' Name I Pray, Amen.

Prayer to Know God and His Power

If you do not know God and want to be connected to or with Him and His resurrection power, than you must say this prayer for salvation.

Father, I come to you in the name of Jesus, I repent of my sins and ask you to forgive me of all my sins. I believe that Jesus died on the cross and shed His blood for the remission of my sins. I ask you now to forgive me of my sins and wash and cleanse me with your blood. Father, I ask Your Son Jesus to come into my heart and be the Lord and Savior of my life. I surrender my spirit, mind, body and soul to you Lord. Now, I believe I am saved according to your word, " That if thou shall confess with thy mouth the Lord

Jesus, and shall believe in thine heart that God has raised Him from the dead, thou shall be saved. For with the heart man believeth unto righteousness, and with the mouth confession is made unto salvation," Romans 9-10.

Prayer for Empowerment of the Holy Spirit

Father, I ask you in the name of Jesus to fill, empower, and manifest your Holy Spirit in my life to succeed with the purpose you have given me. Anoint my business with your spirit of prosperity and success and every business venture I encounter in the world. Lord I am the head and not the tail. Empowerment me with your spirit of wisdom, love, protection, ability, understanding, favor, anointing, and abundant blessing released in my life; over my family, health, business, and over the works of the devil to live a victorious life. Father, I thank you for accepting me as your child into your family and for manifesting and empowering me with your Holy Spirit, so I can speak directly to you in the spirit. I receive my salvation, healing, empowerment and a spirit of restoration for my business. I am set free from the penalty of death, sickness and poverty. Now I can say my business is flourishing like the cedar in Lebanon. Thank you. In Jesus' Name I pray, Amen.

Now you have said these prayers. The next step is to find a good church to worship God and to give your tithes and offering, as in the Bible in Malachi 3:8-12, and a church empowered with the Holy Spirit. Most churches only teach salvation and not how to receive the power of God. Be sure your church teaches both.

Networking in the Local Institution, the Church

The number one need of the local church is getting hold to God's "whole vision" or "plan of salvation," which is inclusive of being economically empowered-financially. The second need of the church is to help people become spiritually and economically empowered-financially in accordance with the scriptures. The Bible

states, "A good man leaveth an inheritance to his children's children; . . . ." (Proverbs 13: 22) Since most Christians' parents or
grandparents did not leave behind anything, but debts to their
children as in II Kings 4:1-7, it is up to the church to assist these
people in establishing wealth by issuing loans and grants for starting businesses. God always had a plan for us because he knew that
businesses created wealth and leadership, but jobs do not. The
Jews always have had money, but for some reason, the protestants
and Catholics did not catch hold of this, because most of them are
workers and not owners. The devil knows that it takes money to
start a business and if a person does not have the money to start a
business, more and likely he would not go into business, but get a
job. This is one of the main reasons why God wants the church to
have access to capital to help the person to start a business. If the
church was acting under God's total "plan of salvation" it would
be in control of the economy by ownership, leadership, power,
and control of the government, media, and lending institutions,
and at least, be able to influence the worldly government on issues
affecting Christians. The people that control and make all the laws
are usually the people in ownership with money. Christians can
pray and call on Jesus, but there comes a time when there is a need
to have money to partake and fulfill the physical needs in the
physical world. Under most circumstances, the Christians should
not have to depend on the world to fulfill their needs because this
should be one of the purposes of the local church, as a governing
organization, to meet the needs of the Saints as in The Acts 6: 1-7.
The early church was wealthy and knew how to care for the Saints
that were in needs, see The Acts 4: 32-35. This is the way the
church should be operated today. The needy Christians should
not have to go to the world banks for loans to start a business,
because the world banks really don't help most of the low-to-mod-
erate families in need, especially, if you are a minority or a woman
or even just being a Christian. Therefore, some how, the church
has to get back into the total business of God since this is a duty to

be handled by the church as a single operating point to take care of all of God 's people and their businesses.

Most of the pastors of churches today do not have God's "whole vision of salvation" at heart. Ministering on Sunday morning is only one small segment of the church's operation and usually the pastors get paid only for providing this service. The deacons and other leaders in the church are not assisting the pastors in the communities because they are busy working on a job and do not have a plan for assisting the pastors. When the deacons are not working on a job, their main duty now is to control the pastor and make sure the money isn't being taken. No wonder the local church is in serious trouble, because this is not God's vision for the church or whole plan of salvation. With all the monies in circulation in the Christian churches, it is **ashamed that there is no vision for a centralized Christian's bank** established in the world to provide capital to Christians. There should be a bank where Christians can go to have access to capital when starting businesses, buying a home, and assisting pastors that are building new churches. Controlling the capital of churches is one of the major steps and vision of God in obtaining economic empowerment for the church in order to have **influence, leadership,** and a **network** to meet the needs of the body. In the older days it was land, and today it is having access to capital.

The third need of the church is being able to network as a single body. All forms of networking should be in existence among the Christians. God is not pleased with the selfishness of man to build his/her own church. Far too many pastors think, since God call them to start the church and they build it from the ground up, they are the boss and the church belong to them. When in fact, it is God's church. In most cases, the pastors try to run the total program, he is the deacon, he is the trustee, and he is the choir. This is because he doesn't know any better or he wants to control the church, but this does not implement God's total program in a church and the church goes lacking of not fulfilling God's "total vision." This is why we have so many churches going up not meeting the needs of God's people, and the pastor wants to say I built this church. A divine call from God to lead His people is serious business. All churches should establish a governing body as in the Bible, I Timothy, Chapter 3. God had twelve disciples (board of Directors) to support him along with other laymen and professional leaders. On the other hand, we find churches operating well and have become a utopia by not having a vision for helping other churches, and this is not of God either. What are pastors doing to sow seed money back into other grassroots churches to help them to be built for the kingdom of God, to help people in their church to improve their lives, and people in their community? Most churches have an International outreach program and this is good, but what about in your community (back yard)? I am not trying to attack the churches nor the pastors, but to shed light on bringing God's "whole vision" on earth that is lacking in the local church.

The church has been and still is as a "whole organization" the most separated and segregated institution on this earth especially in the areas of unity and networking together spiritually and financially in the communities to achieve a common goal of helping Christians to live an abundant life. Many churches today are still dealing with a certain segment of people, which are those people who only come to church services on Sunday morning instead of making an effort to reach out into the community. This may be because many local churches are in the developmental stage and not setup or equipped to meet the basic socio-economic needs of the people. Today, most communities are less personal than they were in the past and the needs have changed with trends. This means that most of the communities are being redeveloped and composed of people of all nationalities, backgrounds, race, and religions with various needs to be met. To operate in the New Millennium, the churches must be equipped and have an active role in the community, and not be self-serving to a select few. If the churches are not involved in the economic development of the community, many churches will not be able to grow and expand to the depth of meeting the spiritual needs and social conditions of all families and at risk youth as God has designed. Charity starts at home and then abroad. To fulfill God's vision, churches should have the following programs in existence to meet the needs of the total person and its community, which are:

- Spiritual Teaching and Ministering

- Financial Support Ministries (credit unions for obtaining loans and grants)

- Investment Program Initiatives

- Financial Counseling for Families

- Youth Ministries that reaches out to Other Youths

- Care Groups

- Children Ministries

- Social Service Ministries

- Housing Program

- Day Care Ministries

- Senior Citizen Ministries

- Community Training and Outreach Programs

- Economic Development Committee

Business Resource Services

The local churches should be one large network with ongoing partnership with other churches of similar creeds and beliefs in the Lord, Jesus Christ. The churches also should network within the local community, with other neighboring communities, corporations, banks, businessmen, local, state, and county officials, neighborhood care groups, nonprofit organizations, and communities leaders to improve the community. Even though the worldly men separate the state from the patronage of religion, God doesn't, neither did our Christian forefathers in leadership, and nor shall we. We, as Christians, should acknowledge God in all things, because it was God through His Son, Jesus, by the Holy Spirit, created the Heaven and Earth and without Him nothing was made, including the people and the government. Therefore, the Church, as a network or an organization, must strive to put Christian men and women in leadership and establish Christian businesses. It is wisdom to keep your spiritual covenant with God and build a strong network with your fellow Christians. It doesn't matter what church you are overseeing on earth if you are in Jesus Christ. We are all connected to one Spirit. A nation is blessed who recognizes its spiritual head. "Blessed is the nation whose God is the Lord; and the people whom he hath chosen for his own inheritance." (Psalms 33:12). Therefore, God's plan is to work through His body (those individuals who confesses Jesus as Lord) to have dominion on earth and bring his plan of salvation into the world.

CHAPTER 5–TEAMING TO OBTAIN WEALTH

Building Financial Partners Relationships is

Wisdom from the Bible

Network Marketing and/or Relationship Marketing

Network Marketing is an alternative method of making a living through relationship. Both network marketing and relationship marketing are a strategic alliance formed by people with the same interest and special needs working together to achieve a special goal or purpose. Network marketing is (1) composed of numbers, (2) volume, and (3) quality. Network marketing strategic alliance marketing teams united, are very strong and powerful if implemented correctly with a plan. The team approach has been known to produce gigantic, extraordinary income for the people involved and produce gigantic and extraordinary sales for company through distribution process. Company views network marketing as one of the best ways to move products and services with a low overhead cost to them and at the same time reward the network marketing teams through commission, overrides and bonuses that would have been paid to a highly trained sale force.

The reason many companies engage in network marketing is because they can contract their services and products to independent contractors through a system known as outsourcing. Network marketing teams are known as independent contractors, distributors, associates, consultants, agents, and so forth. Network marketing is when individuals come together for the same interest and purpose to make money by distributing a company's goods and services as independent contractors.

Network marketing is a group of people or companies merging or joining forces, creating alliances with large companies: such as ATT& T, MCI and WorldCom for one purpose in mind to control and to be the number one companies in the world.

If the larger companies are merging together, why can't the home-based businesses or smaller companies form teams and join forces to compete for the number one position for the small businesses to gain income to achieve the American Dream. Network marketing is a business that strives to help others, which is in agreement with God's word. Nothing can come against a large number of people united for the same interest. For an example, let's look at the strength and power generated from the people of Shem in the Bible when these people decided to build the tower of Babel. "And they said, go to, let us build us a city and a tower, whose top may reach unto heaven; and let us make us a name, unless we be scattered abroad upon the face of the whole earth. And the Lord said, "Behold, the people is one, and they have all one language; and this they begin to do: and now nothing will be restrained from them, which they have imagined to do." (Genesis 11:4, 6) This I believe will happen for network marketing or relationship building when people unite to help each other build a tower of wealth to establish God's Covenant on this earth. I believe small companies; such as TelComNet, Vision, Desktop 2000 and Anderson's Consulting are joining together to achieve the same common goal. Larger companies such as AT&T, MCI, LCI, Bell Atlantic, Sprint, and other 500 fortune companies have made direct/network marketing possible by setting up a system to distribute their products.

My hope is for people to catch the vision and engage in network/relationship marketing. This is one of the reasons this book is written, to educate, teach, and train people. The problem comes when most people have to make a change or an adjustment in their present life situation, and most people don't like to make changes. This is the pitfall of life when too many people allow changes to control them instead of them controlling the changes.

In network marketing, the person is sharing and helping each other to become financially secure more than just for selling. This is the motive behind network marketing and also you can receive the product or service you use free. Most people, however, view network marketing as selling instead seeing it as an invitation to produce alternative income besides working on a job. The concept behind network marketing is to give people an opportunity to produce extraordinary income by using the products and services and sharing them with others. Now, you can eliminate from your mind that network marketing is selling; it is here to help you become financially independent. In other words, you will get paid commission, bonuses, and residual income as long as you use the product. God wants to blessed in abundance, and network marketing is the way I perceive God wants to bless you and others. The church has enough people to create wealth by network marketing without telling members to get a job. There is power in the church to create supernatural wealth that can feed all the members in the church if the church will unite and network together. Whose power is working in the church the world's or God's? Then why do members have to depend on the worldly system?

Network marketing also offers an opportunity for your money to work for you. In most cases in multi-level marketing, everyone must agree to purchase or use a certain amount of product each month so everyone can generate an income. As the organization grows, the more income that is generated by each individual that joins. Remember, I said earlier that money is not meant to accumulate, but to circulate. Most people are not aware of how to generate money that is why they work for money. People must realize that if they want to get out of debt, working on a job is not the answer. If they continue to do the same thing over and over (working on a job), they will get the same thing which is over worked and underpaid, living from paycheck to paycheck, and are barely surviving. This is what has been happening with most people. Not understanding the flow of money. In a free enterprise society, working on a job closes the doors to opportunity of getting out of debt or ever achieving the American Dream.

To illustrate the position of working on a job, think about a box. Do you see the following bondages listed below?

Job

1. Controlled
2. Limitations
3. No way to escape
4. Self-perpetuating
5. Same amount of money earned
6. Fixed income
7. No security
8. Routine

The purpose of using a box is to illustrate growth. There is no room to grow in a box. Owning a business offers you an opportunity to grow, expand, and increase.

Why do you need to Grow? If you don't grow you will die and this is what has happened to a lot of people's dreams and visions by working on a job. A promotion on a job is not the type of growth I am discussing. Therefore, you want to grow and not suffocate in a box. This is what has been happening to people born with gifts and talents and work on a job. The same thing happens with money if you don't use money you will lose it.

To illustration a small business you think of creativity, freedom to choose, and unlimited depths.

Home-based or small business

Is this growth? Yes

Also, it is a Win-Win situation

If you work on a job it violates every principle of a free enterprise society. However, if working on a job is your choice for your life, then you can understand the consequences and why you can't blame anyone else for the status of your life. Or on the other hand, those people, who want to escape this box, can understand why they are in the position and how to overcome it and aim for a better life.

The Power of Strategic Alliance Teams in Networking

Forming Alliance Strategic Teams in Network Marketing is a way to empower people.

The power of forming alliances does not work without leaders. The leaders must possess champion qualities. The champion is the one with the vision and skills to move the alliance forward faster, focused, and aggressive. Champions are exceptional people that you look for in selecting the right choice for your organizations. A champion has these characteristics as defined in John K. Conlon and Melissa Giovagnoli's book "The Power of Two:"

1. *Integrity*–Strong belief or faith to hold the alliance together. Sometimes alliances have to take certain matters on faith. The decision to pursue an opportunity that has not yet emerged– to invest time, people, and money in a venture with no immediate payoff–requires an unshakable belief. This belief isn't always just the venture itself, but in the person leading it. To find out if a person have the integrity to be a champion ask the following questions:

    • Is there any instance in the past when the candidate violated the values or beliefs of the organization?

- Do you feel the candidate would sacrifice a long-term goal for short-term results?

- Is this person basically honest?

- Is he able to work under pressure or throw in the towel when things don't go his/her way?

2. *Strategist*—The ability to think strategically is very much needed to move the business forward. Usually alliance fails because most of them have been created for short-term reasons rather than long ones. In an alliance where team building is needed for an organization to move forward for a long-term must be familiar with the company strategic plan. To find this person these traits must be displayed:

- Knowledge of the organization beyond his or her function.

- Knowledge of where the organization is heading in the next five years.

- A willingness to invest time and resources in a project that may take months to produce an income.

- The ability to analyze what is missing and needed to reach the goals and objectives in terms of technology, people, training, etc.

- The ability to articulate a value proposition clearly and convincingly.

3. *Visionary*—It takes vision to see a future market or trend that other cannot see. It takes courage to express a vision and make commitment to the cause. Champions have this visionary zeal. It's nothing magical but gifted to see how the plan is to be completed and what technology that will affect the business in the future. The visionary possess the following traits:

    •   People who are good about coming up with or constructing scenarios, different alternatives, and possibilities.

    •   Individuals who do their research and data first before putting the vision into process.

    •   Proficient at projecting the impact of an event on numerous parties. The visionary can conceive how an infrastructure network might be put together to take advantage of the scenario.

4. *Planner*–Champions start the alliance off with a plan: (1) making sure the champion at the partner company is involved in shaping it, and (2) they set expectations for the alliance for the first five years. The power of an alliance is rooted in a plan, and the champion is adept at putting one together for the betterment of the company. A planner is responsible for the following:

    •   They help determine the value proposition for the prospective allies to work together.

    •   They help to identify any potential barriers that might prevent the company for succeeding.

    •   They make sure that everyone involved understands the plan.

- The following are characteristics to look for in a planner:

  - Favor specifics over generalities

  - Create effective reports, strategies, and recommendation by working with others as opposed to working alone.

  - Consistently meet deadlines and achieve goals.

  - Are realistic in their expectations rather than pie-in-the-sky dreamers

  - Are good at projecting possibilities and alternatives instead of seeing only one possible scenario.

5. *Communicator*–A champion must be able to get his ideas across clearly and concisely to people that might not "speak his language." Champions transcend these differences. A communicator helps members to recognize the benefits of partnerships to capitalize on an opportunity. A champion can bring these opportunities to life. To find a communicator, look for the following traits:

  - Interact equally well with all ranks of people.

  - Synthesize a variety of opinions and ideas to explain them simply and powerfully.

  - Speak in a way that makes the listener feel as if his or her response counts.

  - Help teams of diverse people understand their mission.

- Persuade people to do things they express initial reluctance about doing.

6. *Collaborator*–This person looks at the long-term relationships and work hard at making sure everyone involved in the alliance benefits. This person is considered as facilitator. The following are the skills that this person must possess:

- Is a talented dealmaker willing to work overtime to make sure an issue is settled?

- Has a background in business development and knows instinctively what to give up in order to get something.

- Focuses on making sure that all parties leave a room feeling as if their goals were met.

- Sees the implications and ramification of decision and factor them in the process.

- Is willing to use any tactic necessary to keep a partnership on track and moving toward its objective.

- Reacts to an exciting new idea or piece of information by sharing it with someone else rather than hoarding it.

7. *Persistence*—a person who is determined to meet the goals and missions. It grows out of a sincere and deep belief in what an alliance stands for and it's ultimate goals. The person beliefs are so strong and persistent no matter how many setbacks and roadblocks occur. The types of skills this person possess are:

- They support an idea they believe in even if it's not politically expedient or they are not in the majority.

- They push for a project consistently even if they've been turned down more than once.

- They are not obnoxious about it, but they keep proposing it until they get a chance to move forward.

- Their persistence is logical and flexible; they push for something only as long as they believe in it, and they're willing to change and adapt their ideas if it gives them a better chance of succeeding.

- They weather criticism and questions well; they don't give up just because a superior expresses skepticism or scorn for their idea.

- They're focused, organized, and know how to complete a task assigned.

- They don't flit from project to project, leaving one behind because a newer and better one appears.

- They are good at concentrating their efforts in support of the concept or recommendation that strikes them as most important.

The main characteristic found in every champion is the ability to be loyal to the cause. A champion believes in what he does and has a strong desire and belief that the vision he or she supports will manifest itself if you can hold strong, have courage, be persistent, and endure long enough. What is loyalty?

Loyalty—A person who will stand with you no matter what whether in a leadership role or follower. This person will support the cause or vision with honesty even when it sees as if the program is falling. This person is very sincere to his cause and is trustworthy. This person is very supportive of your goals, missions, and programs. When everyone else has left the organization, this person will still be there with you. This person might not agree with every thing said or done, but he will carry out the function as presented with dignity and integrity. The Characteristics of this person are:

- Sincere about his work and carry out his duty in the highest esteem.

- Easy to get along with and does very little talking with opposite.

- Very orderly and organized person. Always helping or fixing something.

- Feel very positive about the cause or purpose.

- Willingness to do all things that will increase the betterment of the organization. This person does not gossip or speak against his leader to any body in the staff. Mostly this person is negative when opposition arrives and still present when it is over.

- This person is patient and respects the leader in the highest. Does not try to take over or control the business. You can always count on this person.

America is a Land of Opportunities

A Free Enterprise Society

This means that in America everyone has an equal opportunity to have the rights to control its life's destiny through entrepreneurship, because a free enterprise system supports a person who dares to dream and does all they can to get that dream to come to past.

America is a Nation that is built under God, and this Nation's Principle of free enterprise is in line with the word of God. This allows individuals to exercise their gifts and talents to achieve their God-given purpose in life to help each other. Remember the Lord our God it is He who gives us power to get wealth so that His Covenant can be established on this earth. Deut 8:18.

Network Marketing, I believe, is God's plan to distribute wealth opportunity to every American to fulfill their Dream for those who catch the vision, run the race, and invest.

In this New Millennium, everything is a network, and this age is conducive to individuals getting involved with networking and network marketing companies. The traditional ways of doing busy will be decrease tremendous and some things will disappeared in its entirely all except for service jobs. The Computer Age or Network Age with "the Internet" has changed the way people will work and how businesses will be conducted in the future. Do not try to hold onto the past. This is a time to change your life. The time to have an abundant life has never been greater as an entrepreneur.

CHAPTER 6–DIRECT SELLING STATISTICS

How Do I Know Network Marketing Work?

Network marketing will work because the timing for network marketing to peak is now. Network marketing has worked in the past and will continue to work in the future because of the growing demand presented by the technology movement. Technology will create a need for this type of marketing service. More and more people will be using the Internet to do business from their home due to the high corporate layoffs of jobs that will never return. During business by network marketing and from the Internet will cause many stores to go out of business due to the high level of buying on the web. As we move into the New Millennium, more people would be forced to get involve with network marketing even though some people have had bad experiences in building an organization. The term "marketing" has always been a way to get the products and services to the customers at the best and lowest overall cost. The Internet and network marketing have proven to be a successful marketing tool to reach many consumers. This saves the companies money in advertisement and distribution. In the 21st century it will not be a matter of whether network marketing works, it will be a matter of who is marketing from each other first will be the name of the game. Are you marketing to your friends or are your friends marketing to you? What you want to do is to get involved now and be the first to build a network so when the network explosion come you would already be established. Instead of you paying others, they will be paying you. I hope this book has changed your outlook on things and helped you to put into effect the principles or intent to change your life. I invite you to join the millions of people involved in direct/network marketing and/or multilevel marketing who are working only four-hour days and earning extraordinary income.

Should you consider network marketing as a business, e-mail us at telcomnet@hotmail.com. Visit our web site at **www.telcomnetinc.com**. Any questions should be referred to TeleComNet, Inc., refer to Teampower Operation, at (703) 750-3544, and we will help you to form a company to move beyond your present economic status of living from paycheck to paycheck to prosperity.

Facts and Statistics about Direct Selling

The Direct Selling Association Foundation, located in Washington, DC, is a recognized trade association for direct selling channel of distribution, shows some of the following statistics:

1. An estimated $24.54 billion in retail sales in the United States in 1999. Today this figure will rise rapidly, since more and more people understand direct selling, multilevel, and network marketing and connecting their sales increase to the Internet.
2. Demographics of people involved in Networking Marketing Sales Force.

    •Independent contractors
    •Female/male/couples
    •Professionals
    •Technical people
    •Housewives

3. Services and Products involved in Direct Sales Groups.

- Home/family care products (cleaning and cutlery, etc.)
- Personal care products (cosmetics, jewelry, skin care, etc)
- Services (telecommunications, utility, wireless, etc.)
- Hygiene and health products (weight loss, vitamins, water, etc.)
- Leisure/educational products (books, encyclopedias, toys, games, etc.)
- Oil, (gasoline, etc.)

4. Sales Strategy

- Individual (door-to-door selling, usually one-to-one)
- Conference calling
- Group selling
- Internet selling
- Trade shows selling
- Seminars/meetings
- Networking clubs
- Friends
- referrals
- Others

To obtain more information on statistics concerning direct selling call Direct Selling Association at (202) 347-8866 or see their web site at www.dsa.org.

Business Questions and Concerns

Question: What is the different between a network marketing business and a regular small business?

Answer: Network marketing usually requires less effort and time operating it, than working on a business. People help people earn income through teaming and leveraging. Most people have gotten use to routine and to get involve in a network marketing company it is a lot of fun. It is mostly recruiting and using the services or products.

Question: Do I need a Business Plan or Market Plan?

Answer: Yes. A business plan includes the market plan. It is used to display vision of your business similar to a road map. It tells you how to get to where you want to go. It serves as a blueprint of how you plan to put your idea into reality.

Question: I am shy and I cannot communicate with others will I have to speak to groups? And what other qualifications I need to start a business?

Answer: No. There are others that will speak to groups for you. Starting a business takes less time and qualifications to set up: None

Question: Are jobs secure? Will I be able to depend on a job?

Answer: No, not all jobs are secure. Jobs have always been in existence and will continue to be in existence. They have always served as a temporary means of making a living. Temporary means that when you exalt all of your annual or sick leave on a job, you do not get paid. Also due to the technology movement, most of the high paying traditional jobs will be reengineered or abolished. The electronics age will create fewer demands for people to perform jobs as they once did in the past. The future jobs will be through hi-tech paying jobs created by entrepreneurs. The future for jobs will be unpredictable unless they are services oriented. We are going to see many jobs up today and gone tomorrow due to the rapid change in technology.

Question: The technology movement is moving so fast. How can I keep up with the changes occurring in the world today?

Answer: By reading books and learning to use the computer will keep you up-to-date about changes taking place on the Internet. Also, by enrolling in various workshops in your neighborhood.

Question: Since I am a Christian, I want to know will God take care of me?

Answer: Yes. The promises are ye and amen to only those who hear God and are preparing themselves. God always warns and gives you directions as to what you are to do. Are you hearing from God? Are you taking time to get to know God by reading your Bible? Are you obeying and giving tithes and offering?

Question: Why is it important to take control of your financial needs?

Answer: Because when someone looks after your interest, they have a plan in mind to control you for their own gain. We need to be less dependent on the world's system and the government as much as possible.

Network Marketing Nonprofit Lobbying Groups

Listed are the Top 20 Power Network Marketing Lobbying Groups with the most clout in Washington, DC, on Capitol Hill.

1. American Association of Retired Persons
2. American Israel Public Affairs Committee
3. National Federation of Independent Business
4. Nation Rifle Association of America
5. AFL-CIO

6. Association of Trail Lawyers of America
7. Christian Coalition
8. Credit Union National Association
9. National Right to Life Committee
10. American Medical Association
11. Chamber of Commerce
12. Independent Insurance Agents of America
13. National Association of Manufacturers
14. American Farm Bureau Federation
15. National Restaurant Association
16. National Association of Home Builder
17. National Association of Realtors
18. National Association of Broadcasters
19. Motion Picture Association of America
20. American Bankers Association

Powerful Network Organizations

Others network Organizations that are powerful because of the teaming concept.

NFL Football

NFL Basketball

Hockey

Girl Scouts

Dry Cleaner Association

American Bible Society

Others Financial Organizations:

Amway

May Kay

American Communication Network

Excel Communications

Banks–Large Corporations

CHAPTER 7–BUSINESS SAVVY

Entrepreneur Test—

Test Your Desire to Start a Business

The "Average home-based business income is $50,250 a year, and twenty percent of home business owners earn over $100,000 a year." This figure might have increased now.

Source–American Home Business Association.

Do You Have What It Takes to Run a Successful Home Based Business?

1. Do you want a better quality of life for you and your family? _____

2. Are you satisfied with your present economic status?_____

3. Are you willing to work longer or harder in a business then you do now if it means that your life will be different? _____

4. Are you self-motivated? _____

5. Do you need someone else to show you how to organize and direct your time?_____

6. Would you prefer to achieve your highest financial goals by owning your own business or working on a job to help someone achieve their goals? _____

7. Do you feel that you can reach financial independence by working for someone else or working for yourself in a your own business?_____

8. Do you prefer working for someone else on a job than being your own boss?_____

9. Do you think you have the knowledge and ability needed to start and operate a business?_____

10. Given an opportunity to operate a business to purchase an already existing business, do you feel that you can take the business and operate it?_____

11. Do you think that owning a business always mean longer hours?_____

12. Are you willing to do something different to change your present job status?_____

13. Are you just afraid to start a business?_____

14. Is getting money to start your business one of your obstacle? _____

15. Do you know where you can get the money from to start a business?_____

16. Would you like to play a larger role in your own destiny?_____

17. Are you contented to let others determine your destiny?_____

18. Do you desire to help people achieve their destiny?_____

19. Do you have a vision of what you want to do in life and how to obtain it?_____

20. Do you think Network Marketing creates more responsibility than any other business?_____

21. Score?

18-20 -You are an entrepreneur and probably already own your business.

15-17 You have strong entrepreneurial characteristics.

12-14 You have a good foundation to build on.
With training and assistance, you can succeed in business.

11-less–You are probably not ready to go into business for yourself. You need greater awareness, education, and desire in this area.

PROFILE OF CHOICE

YOUR MIND SET DETERMINES YOUR LIFE

A—PLAN WORLD'S ECONOMIC SYSTEM	B—PLAN GOD'S ECONOMIC SYSTEM
GO TO COLLEGE	PLANT A SEED II Corinthians 9:6 & 10
GET A JOB	PAY TITHES/ SELF-EMPLOYED (Malachi 3:10 & Leviticus: 27:30)
BONDAGE/CONTROLLED	REPRODUCE/ MULTIPLY (II Corinthians 9:8-12)
GET CREDIT CARD	USE AS IDENTIFICATION (Prov.22: 1 & I Corinthians 2:12)
30-YEAR DEBT ON HOUSE	PAY OFF HOUSE IN CASH (Proverb 12:22 &13:22)
BORROW	LEND (II Kings 4:1-7 & Proverbs 22:7)

RD

WORK FOR YOUR MONEY	YOUR MONEY WORKS FOR YOU/INVESTMENTS (Matt. 25:14-30/I Peter 5:7)

Notes:

1. Plan B above is based on the Biblical plan of God.
2. Most people start their life with Plan A above, then advance to Plan B above.
3. We recommend getting a college education to obtain knowledge and skill, but the key to financial secure is working for yourself upon completing college. College alone does not create financial independence.

Comparison of Working on a Job vs. Owning a Network Marketing Business (NMB)

A Job Plan	NMB
THE WORLD'S SYSTEM	*GOD'S ECONOMIC SYSTEM*
Work 40 to 50 YEARS	Work 2 to 5 YEARS
Post-Retirement	Enjoy Life
No time to enjoy life	
AVG PERSON WORKS 45 YEARS	AVG PERSON WORKS 2 1/2 YRS
45 WKS/YR	40 WKS/YR
1,800 HRS/YR	400 HRS/YR
81,000 HRS/CAREER	2,000 HRS/CAREER
RETIRE—1/3 INCOME	RETIRE—INCOME GROWING
FIXED INCOME	RESIDUAL INCOME
(Stops)	(Continuous)
PAY MORE TAXES	RECEIVE TAX DEDUCTIONS
UNSTABLE EMPLOYMENT	SECURED EMPLOYMENT

WORK FOR SELF	HELP SELF AND OTHERS
WORK FOR MONEY	LIVE GOD'S PURPOSE IN LIFE
TEMPORARY INCOME	PERMANENT INCOME
STRUGGLING	ABUNDANCE

THIS IS NOT JUST A PLAN. THIS IS ABOUT YOUR LIFE.

YOUR SUCCESS IS WITHIN YOU

*YOU MUST MAKE
A CHOICE TO CONTROL YOUR OWN DESTINY*

WHICH PLAN WILL YOU CHOOSE FOR YOUR LIFE?

LIFEPLAN

Career Check List

(Answer All Questions)

1. If you have a job when would you like to retire from it?

    In three years
    In five years
    In ten years
    In twenty years
    In thirty years

    How do you plan to achieve this goal?
    Answer:

RD

2. How much money do you plan to be making monthly when you retire?
   $1,000
   $4,000
   $5,000
   $8,000 OR MORE

   What you plan to do to receive this monthly income?
   Answer:

3. Do you plan to invest some of the money you receive?

   Where do you plan to invest your money?
   Answer:

4. What is your present work status?

   Do you own or plan to start a business?
   What types of business and what is hindering you from starting your own business?

The Making of Millionaires through TeamPower 777 Networking

The Network of the Future

This is the strategic Plan God laid on my heart to implement to help people obtain wealth through entrepreneurship. The vehicle or system used is known as TeamPower networking, which is designed to help people overcome all the pitfalls problems connected to network marketing as discussed in this book. TeamPower networking is God's plan for people who are crying out for financial freedom and are hesitating about starting their own business due to having the funds. Some people are looking for an opportunity to escape the American job trap, but need leaders and a sound plan with structure or substance to execute. Networking will grow tremendously after reading this book because people will understand its purpose, have more trust in network marketing. TelComNet, Inc. offers business services to assist, educate, and help people's get involve in business venture. If you are not a part of a network, we invite you to get involve with TeamPower networking.

More information concerning the Teampower Network can be obtained by writing to:
TelComNet
P.O. Box 50
Annandale, VA 22003
Email: *telcomnet@hotmail.com*
Internet Address: www.telcomnetinc.com (Send all requests)
(703) 256-5760 (FAX)

Wisdom Financially for Everyday Living

Having Wisdom About Money

God said "for the love of money is the root of all evil, which, while some coveted after, they have erred from the faith, and pierced themselves through with many sorrow." (1 Timothy 6:10). What God is saying in this passage is that the love of money is the root of all evil, not having money. God himself created money for his children to have on this earth. It is not a sin to talk about or have money when we work eight hours or more a day for money. We spend eight hours a day or a lifetime working for money to survive on earth. All our physical resources depend upon having money—our houses, clothes, food, etc. Therefore, to talk about money, it doesn't necessary cause a person to be evil, operate in greed and lust, or love money.

To not have or talk about money is a trick of the devil to deceive you, so he can control your life. The devil wants to control the children of God by making them feel guilty or condemned by talking about money. Today, many Christians get offended or fearfully when they or you talk about money. I want you to know that it is okay to talk about money and to have money, because God created money for his people. The Christians do not magnify God when they are not prosperous, Psalms 35:27. Christians can never be the witnesses that God wants them to be as long as they are in bondage to the world's economic system. God's word states in Deuteronomy 8:18 "Remember the Lord our God it is he who give us power to get wealth so we can establish his covenant on earth." God gives us vision and wisdom to create wealth through our talents and special gifts. Therefore, to be afraid or offended when someone talks about money should not be the case when we need it for survival. We must operate in faith as a child of God to create tangible thing into this earthly realm. Faith comes from hearing and hearing and hearing the word of God. If money is never mentioned, you can never hear faith to confess money into existence on earth to live an abundant life and help others. Most people who get offended by talking about money lack knowledge of the word of God of how confession of words by faith creates reality. The word of God states in Ecclesiastes 9:16 "the poor man's wisdom is despised, and his words are not heard." This simply means that no one will listen to a poor man and for Christians to get anything from God, it must be through an act faith.

The problem with most of God's children is that they are not renewing their minds financially according to God's word or plan for them to follow on this earth. "And be not conformed to this world, but be ye transformed by the renewing of your mind that you may prove what is good and acceptable, and perfect will of God." (Romans 12:2) This means to know the perfect will for your life financially. It is definitely not God's will for Christians to be working on a job because this conforms to the world's system. When you work on a job you are a servant under an unsaved person who controls your productive years of your life (12 to 14 hours a day). The only time you have left after a day's work is to go to bed, sleep, and back to your job the next morning. This is not what God intended for his children. This is bondage and slavery, and it makes a person to be the tail, and not the head. The word of God tells us that we should be the head and not the tail. God tells us this in His word because He wants us to understand that the devil has a plan for our life too. The devil's plan is for you to fail and be the tail from birth to death, which is to complete high school and college and work on a job for him for the rest of your life until you retire. Then the devil tries to control your post-retirement by having you to get a job after you retire. This is why I believe, most people work on a job because their minds are pro-grammed to think as the world. God has a plan for His children to live an abundant life as part of our inheritance. This is why God's told us to renew our mind and don't be conformed to this worldly system including working on a job. We can't obtain God's benefits and overcome our financial difficulties if we don't apply His principles. Isaiah states "...And you labor for that, which satisfieth not? Hearken diligently unto me, and eat that which is good, and let your soul delight itself in fatness." We need to get a spiritual awakening of self-employment, so we can be blessed. Paying tithes on Sunday Morning does not automatically create wealth without being mixed with action and faith according to Matthew 25:14:30. We must plant a seed (investment some of our money) to reach a harvest and stop eating all your seed money received. Invest in something or start a business to get free of your debt and liability. You know something is wrong with working if you have been work-ing all these years and the things you have to show are debt and liability. Then you know it is insanity to keep working on a job and expecting to get out of debt when it causes you to have more debt.

Wisdom Behind Financial Services

Most people are impartial and afraid about borrowing money to start a business or use other people's money (OPM) other than to buy a house, a car, or charge merchandise on credit cards. God wants everyone to be able to afford any thing in life without borrowing. So what is the secret of getting out of debt and taking advantage of the financial system? Putting your money and other people's money to work for you.

God's word says the wealth of the wicked is laid up for the just. If you have been using your money to pay your bills, living by pay check-to-check; or if you don't have any money to put into a cash flow system to accumulate wealth, then use other people money to get seed money to invest in a business. If you are skeptical about a business to invest your money, then contact the TelComNet, Inc. They will help you. There are many doors and opportunities open for you, but the key is finding the right door that has been opened for you. There are very few people I know who have ever started a business without some financial assistance. Most people simply take a step of faith mixed with OPM money.

Other Books By the Author

Breaking the Financial Curse of Poverty Over Your Life—Entrepreneurship: A Divine Calling from God co-authored with Dr. Betty Lancaster-Short.

A Simple Guide to Understanding the Federal Income Tax Regulations as They Apply To Churches.

Federal Income Taxes and The Small Business Person (A simple

Guide to Understanding Key Elements of the Tax Law as It Relates to Successfully Starting and Operating a Small Business).

24-Hour Global Intercessory Prayer

Pamphlet: How to Build a Nonprofit Business

To order books by the author

Go to: *www.quicksitemaker.com*/members/rubyw

Special Notice–Charitable Organization Supported

A portion of the net proceeds will be donated to one of the following Charitable Organizations below:

   a.   Families United for Restoration
   b.   Youth for Life
   c.   Economic Empowerment Foundation for Women
   d.   Independent Living for Senior citizens

If you would like to make a charity donation to Families United for Restoration (FUR), see our web site at: *www.familyunitedforrestoration.org* It is a 501(c) 3 tax exempt organization to help low–moderate families and at risk youth.

Telephone No. for FUR is (703) 750-3544

About the Author

Dr. Ruby Ward has been a successful licensed and ordained minister and spiritual leader for many people seeking to change their life spiritually and financially.

She is married, has two children, and five grandchildren.

She is the founder and Director of Families United for Restoration, and the Economic Empowerment Foundation for Women. Both programs are community-based organizations to assist families (men, women, and children) spiritually and financially.

She was inspired to write this book because of the lack of information today pertaining to alternative opportunities of making a living besides working on a job to have a successful life.

This book teaches people how to take control financially over their lives by applying spiritual principles and taking physical action.

The author focuses on helping mankind to live a successful life. In all of her books she creates an atmosphere where you can obtain Godly wisdom and understanding as it relates to a person's life.

She has written several best selling books to help people understand God's plan for their life spiritually, financially, and socioeconomically.

She teaches economic empowerment.

Most people see the author as a true woman of God making a difference in other lives and one who understands her true potentiality in life.

Many people have read her books and applied her teaching to their life.

The author teaches that "your life is changing whether you are involved or not." Don't work all of your life for someone else's dreams and still can't afford to retire.

Summary of Book

This book illuminates ideas for new ventures in the changing job market. The author urges the readers to rethink the commonly accepted conventions of wage earning and boldly embrace the new entrepreneurial opportunities opening up in the new technological age. She offers exciting ideas for finding a career that puts your money in circulation to work for you, instead of you working for your money. Never before has the concept of business networking been more practical as the Internet puts the marketplace in your home and at your fingertips. *"Escaping the American Job Trap,"* offers a practical plan and proven strategies for establishing a home-based "system" through a direct multilevel marketing business that will free you from the constraints, insecurities and limitations of a traditional job. Well-researched, informative and communicated in a friendly, accessible voice. The author has written another book that offers creative financial opportunities for Christians, *"Breaking the Financial Curse of Poverty Over Your Life.—Entrepreneurship: A Divine Calling From God."*

She states plainly that the "key" to financial independence in life is not going to be through a job, but to get purged into an opportunity "system" offering a financial vision to change your future. If you can't find a system, then create your own.